Effec

fo

WITHDRAWN

FROM THE LIBRARY OF
UNIVERSITY OF ULSTER

www.skills4study.com

rs   *Joan van Emden*

avy

Effective   Arts and Humanities Students   *Joan van Emden and Lucinda Becker*
Effective Communication for Science and Technology   *Joan van Emden*
How to Manage your Arts, Humanities and Social Science Degree   *Lucinda Becker*
How to Manage your Science and Technology Degree   *Lucinda Becker and David Price*
How to Write Better Essays   *Bryan Greetham*
Key Concepts in Politics   *Andrew Heywood*
The Mature Student's Guide to Writing   *Jean Rose*
Making Sense of Statistics   *Michael Wood*
The Postgraduate Research Handbook   *Gina Wisker*
Professional Writing   *Sky Marsen*
Research Using IT   *Hilary Coombes*
Skills for Success   *Stella Cottrell*
The Student's Guide to Writing   *John Peck and Martin Coyle*
The Study Skills Handbook (second edition)   *Stella Cottrell*
Study Skills for Speakers of English as a Second Language   *Marilyn Lewis and Hayo Reinders*
Studying Economics   *Brian Atkinson and Susan Johns*
Studying History (second edition)   *Jeremy Black and Donald M. MacRaild*
Studying Mathematics and its Applications   *Peter Kahn*
Studying Modern Drama (second edition)   *Kenneth Pickering*
Studying Psychology   *Andrew Stevenson*
Teaching Study Skills and Supporting Learning   *Stella Cottrell*

Palgrave Study Guides: Literature

General Editors: John Peck and Martin Coyle

How to Begin Studying English Literature (third edition)   *Nicholas Marsh*
How to Study a Jane Austen Novel (second edition)   *Vivien Jones*
How to Study Chaucer (second edition)   *Rob Pope*
How to Study a Charles Dickens Novel   *Keith Selby*
How to Study Foreign Languages   *Marilyn Lewis*
How to Study an E. M. Forster Novel   *Nigel Messenger*
How to Study James Joyce   *John Blades*
How to Study Linguistics (second edition)   *Geoffrey Finch*
How to Study Modern Poetry   *Tony Curtis*
How to Study a Novel (second edition)   *John Peck*
How to Study a Poet (second edition)   *John Peck*
How to Study a Renaissance Play   *Chris Coles*
How to Study Romantic Poetry (second edition)   *Paul O'Flinn*
How to Study a Shakespeare Play   *John Peck and Martin Coyle*
How to Study Television   *Keith Selby and Ron Cowdery*
Linguistic Terms and Concepts   *Geoffrey Finch*
Literary Terms and Criticism (third edition)   *John Peck and Martin Coyle*
Practical Criticism   *John Peck and Martin Coyle*

Effective Communication for Arts and Humanities Students

Joan van Emden and Lucinda Becker

palgrave
macmillan

100471645
808.066
VAN

© Joan van Emden and Lucinda Becker 2003

All rights reserved. No reproduction, copy or transmission of this publication may be made without written permission.

No paragraph of this publication may be reproduced, copied or transmitted save with written permission or in accordance with the provisions of the Copyright, Designs and Patents Act 1988, or under the terms of any licence permitting limited copying issued by the Copyright Licensing Agency, 90 Tottenham Court Road, London W1T 4LP.

Any person who does any unauthorised act in relation to this publication may be liable to criminal prosecution and civil claims for damages.

The authors have asserted their rights to be identified as the authors of this work in accordance with the Copyright, Designs and Patents Act 1988.

First published 2003 by
PALGRAVE MACMILLAN
Houndmills, Basingstoke, Hampshire RG21 6XS and
175 Fifth Avenue, New York, N.Y. 10010
Companies and representatives throughout the world

PALGRAVE MACMILLAN is the global academic imprint of the Palgrave Macmillan division of St. Martin's Press, LLC and of Palgrave Macmillan Ltd. Macmillan® is a registered trademark in the United States, United Kingdom and other countries. Palgrave is a registered trademark in the European Union and other countries.

ISBN 0–333–98487–0 paperback

This book is printed on paper suitable for recycling and made from fully managed and sustained forest sources.

A catalogue record for this book is available from the British Library.

A catalog record for this book is available from the Library of Congress.

10   9   8   7   6   5   4   3   2   1
12   11   10   09   08   07   06   05   04   03

Printed in China

This book is dedicated to the memory of
Wolfgang van Emden
1931–2002

Contents

Preface   x

Part One: Introduction   1

1 At the Beginning of Your Course   3
Studying effectively   5
First assignment   7
Writing and speaking   9

Part Two: Writing Skills   11

2 Listening, Reading and Making Notes   13
Listening   13
Reading lists   17
Reading skills   17
Making notes   25
Recording information from printed sources   28
Formats for notes   31
Notes from the Internet and similar sources   32

3 Essays, Reports and Dissertations   36
Essays   36
Reports   50
Dissertations   55
Revision and checking   66

4 Good Writing Style   69
Appropriate writing   70
Words   74

Punctuation   80
Sentences   88
Paragraphs   92
Active or passive?   92
Inclusive language   93
Listening to language   94

Part Three: Speaking Skills   95

5 Small-group Presentations   97
Seminars   98
Tutorials   104

6 Formal Presentations   106
Preparing your material   107
Notes   111
Visual aids as notes   115
Note cards   116
Timing the presentation   118
Handouts   119
Visual aids   120

7 Delivery and Non-verbal Communication   132
First appearances   132
Using your nerves   135
Using your voice effectively   137
Non-verbal communication (body language)   141
Using humour   146
Answering questions   147
Shared presentations   148
Improving your presentation skills   149

Part Four: Assessment Methods   151

8 Assessment, Revision and Exam Techniques   153
Assessment   153
Revision   156
Exam techniques   158
Vivas   162

Part Five: Applying for a Job   165

9   Preparing a Job Application and CV   167
   Application forms   168
   The curriculum vitae   175
   The covering letter   179
   Online applications   182
   Example CV and covering letter   183
   Research proposals   187

10 The Successful Job Interview   190
   Careers fairs and similar occasions   191
   The telephone interview   194
   The first interview   195
   The second interview   200

Further Reading   206
Index   207

Preface

Increasingly, communication skills are included in arts and humanities courses at universities and colleges, not as an optional extra but as an integral and assessed part of a student's work. Employers, too, are interested in a potential employee's ability to absorb huge amounts of information, and to write and speak clearly and convincingly.

This book guides students through the main forms of communication which they will need in order to follow their courses successfully and get jobs at the end. The authors discuss tasks such as reading efficiently and taking notes from lectures, books and the Internet – skills often overlooked or taken for granted by lecturers and tutors. Help is given with writing essays, reports and dissertations, and with leading seminars, giving presentations and making the most of tutorials. Finally, the student is guided through the important tasks of writing application forms and CVs, and succeeding at job interviews.

Each stage is discussed in a friendly and informal way, with examples from a range of subjects in the arts and humanities. We are very grateful to the students who, either deliberately or by accident, have given us useful material to illustrate both good and bad practice.

We would especially like to thank the late Emeritus Professor Wolfgang van Emden and Dr Wendy Gibson of the Department of French Studies at the University of Reading for their valuable help and advice, and our colleagues Elizabeth Barber and Anne Pinnock for useful information and the regular support they have given us. We are also grateful to Anastasia and Felicity Becker, whose careful work on the index was invaluable. Any mistakes that remain are our own.

Joan van Emden
Lucinda Becker
Reading, 2003

Part One
Introduction

1 At the Beginning of Your Course

Traditionally, it's been assumed that we can all communicate. We speak, we listen and, from a very early age, we read and write. Why should we need to be trained in, or read books about, such topics? These may be general human activities, but that doesn't mean that we're very good at them. In the past few years, communication has become very much more sophisticated; think of the means by which we receive and pass on information: the telephone, email, fax, seminars, videoconferencing, for a start. There are more possibilities for communication than our grandparents ever dreamed of – and more opportunities for things to go wrong.

The transition from school to higher education highlights some of the problems. It can be exhilarating, but it can also be intimidating. You no longer have a tightly structured day that you are more or less compelled to follow; the amount of work you do is largely your concern and nobody else's; and you have new responsibilities, such as accommodation, food and budgeting to consider. In addition to all this, you have the communication: you have to face large libraries, lectures, tutorials and other strange sources of information, and you may be expected to produce work in what may be new forms, such as notes, essays and seminars. Even if you have experience of these from school, there's the initial doubt: will an essay as I wrote it at school be acceptable at this level?

If you are a mature student, or studying part time, you will have additional responsibilities which will not go away just because you're studying. Your family may rightly have the first claim on your time; you will presumably have discussed the situation with them and obtained their support long before you arrive at university or college. Nevertheless, neither they nor you could have foreseen exactly how your student life will be organized, and you will need to keep them fully informed during the first critical weeks of adjustment. Staff are generally well aware of the extra difficulties that mature students face and are likely to be supportive, but you especially can't afford to get behind with your work and will need to plan your time carefully. If this sounds daunting, remember that a lecturer is usually delighted to have mature students in a class, and you may have much to give in terms of your experience of family life and work.

Most students nowadays have some kind of part-time work to help their finances, but if you are holding down a full-time job or working a large number of part-time hours, you have similar problems and advantages to those of other mature students. You must organize your time in consultation with your employer and agree a sensible work plan, but be ready to adjust this as you settle into your course of study.

All mature students, with either family ties or work responsibilities or both, are likely to get extremely tired and at the same time have less time available for study. Accept this and try not to resent it. You also have a maturity of outlook and a sense of proportion which a young student straight from school is unlikely to have, and these are enormous advantages. You may also be used to concentrating on the task in hand and at the same time balancing several conflicting demands on your time. As long as you don't undermine your health by inadequate sleep and recreation, you have much to offer and much to gain from embarking on a course of study.

> *Key point: if you are a mature student, you have much to offer, but you need to plan your time and relaxation with particular care.*

Help is usually given to all new students, of course, by lecturers, tutors and library staff, who are very aware of the stress that so many new experiences can generate, but the amount of individual help varies between colleges, universities, faculties and departments; it may also depend on the student knowing what and whom to ask. Many of the problems that the new student faces are beyond the scope of this book, but others, involving aspects of communication, are often overlooked: reading efficiently and making notes, for instance.

The aspects of communication discussed in this book involve skills which can be learnt and practised, in conditions that make study both congenial and challenging. You have some responsibility for the conditions in which you work, and that is why, first of all, we look at ways in which new students can help themselves to study successfully.

▶ Studying effectively

This is not a book about how to study (there are plenty of those), but one which will give you help with producing and organizing information; it will be invaluable as you start to prepare your assignments and throughout your course. But before you begin such preparation, it's worth looking briefly at the physical conditions in which you will be studying, and thinking how you can make them comfortable and at the same time conducive to concentrated effort. Where and how can you study most effectively?

You'll be spending a great deal of your time receiving information, and this activity will take place initially in lecture rooms or lecture theatres; we'll discuss the tasks of listening and taking notes in Chapter 2. Where will you carry out your own work? In order to gather material, you may need a library, either the main university or college library or a smaller – and probably less intimidating – library in your faculty or department. Visit the libraries which you are most likely to need, early in your course; try to locate one or two books or journals which you already know about from school or a first lecture, just so that you begin to find your way around; ask a member of the library staff for help if you need it. You may meet a dedicated subject librarian, an expert in your own area of study, who will help you throughout your course.

The library isn't just about books and journals: it's likely to provide a range of services which will be useful to you. Some material, such as journals, will almost certainly be available online, and the library may also provide you with Internet access. Most large libraries run short courses in useful topics such as study or IT skills and advice on the preparation of visual aid material. There may be a resource room fitted out with the latest technology which you can book in order to try out PowerPoint or rehearse a presentation. Your library will be a learning centre which will help and support you throughout your course, and it's a good idea to find out exactly what is available as soon as you can.

You may be fortunate enough to have a guided tour of all these library facilities to help you familiarize yourself with the resources you will need, but it would be a good idea to revisit the library by yourself soon after such a tour, so that you begin to feel at ease there when you are alone. Choose a good place to sit and read, not near the door, where you will be distracted by other people, and not by a window if it's a warm day. Perhaps you can find a book which will give you a general introduction to study, as this one does, or a brief introduction to your subject. Read for a short while, until you are familiar with the atmosphere of the building. Browse around to get the feel of the areas which will be of use to you: find out where journals in your subject, current and back issues, are stored; check the computer and photocopying facilities. It will soon cease to feel strange.

Key point: familiarize yourself with the library and its resources, asking for advice when you need it.

In September or October, you may have a good deal of choice about where you sit in the library; as exam time approaches, you'll find that there is little free space and a queue for any facility you need. More than ever, you'll need somewhere else to prepare your assignments. This will probably be a room at home, in hall or in a shared flat. Make sure from the start that you have a space which is yours, and if you have to share a room, that you and your roommate agree early on about times when there is quiet and when visitors are not welcome. You have work to do!

In order to concentrate, you'll need a desk or table and a chair which is the right height for you. You will also need a good, directed light. Few central lights are sufficient for reading and a small table lamp is essential. You may choose to have two chairs, one more comfortable, in which you can read, and another which is upright, giving you as much back support as possible when you are writing or using a computer. Physical discomfort is a great distraction.

For the same reason, it's not a good idea to work for very long stretches of time without a break. You will feel stiff and your eyes will get tired. Plan your day and include time for fresh air and exercise, after which you'll work more effectively. Meet other students – not only those who are studying the same subjects – and join clubs and societies. Give yourself the sleeping time which is right for you; you probably already know whether you are a 'lark', working best in the mornings, or an 'owl', who works best late at night. Don't try to be both for long periods of time.

When you are working, you may like to have music to listen to, perhaps using a Discman. If this helps you to concentrate, it does no harm, but do remember that you will have silence in the exam room, and if you are too accustomed to sound, its sudden absence can be unnerving. So do some of your work in silence, so that it always seems natural to you. For a similar reason, you should not always write on a computer; using a pen can seem strange and almost unnatural if you are used to a keyboard, and you will be writing by hand in your exams. You may also find that in this way you think more carefully of the exact message you want to convey; easy editing on the computer can result in careless writing.

During your study time, stop for short breaks, a cup of coffee for instance, and within your reading time, look up from the page or the screen every few minutes to allow your eyes to refocus: this will take only a few seconds, but it will help you to concentrate and avoid eye strain.

Above all, try to keep to a regular pattern of work. If you get behind, it will be hard to catch up and you may start to panic as exams approach. Discuss your work with one or two friends, especially if you found some ideas difficult: if you all have the same problem, then go together to the lecturer concerned and ask for help – straightaway, not the day before the exam. Make a practice of handing in work on time; not only will this help you to get better grades as there will be a penalty for late work, but it also means that if there is an acceptable reason for lateness, such as being ill, you'll meet sympathy and help rather than disbelief!

Key point: make your working environment as helpful as possible: good lighting, reasonable comfort and a sensible work pattern.

▶ First assignment

You will soon be given your first assignment, notes, an essay or similar. If you receive no guidance about its length, ask – it's much easier to plan if you know what the constraints are. It's also worth considering what the objectives of the lecturer are. Almost certainly, he or she wants to know how much you already understand about the subject; it's not much use simply copying out your lecture notes. Can you think independently, give a reasoned opinion? Can you assimilate your notes and reading, and have you taken the time to look up any reference which has been drawn to your attention? The lecturer is assessing you, not so much in terms of what sort of qualification you will get at the end of the course, but in terms of how much explanation the class as a whole needs, how familiar they are with the terms used and perhaps what potential there is among the group.

This approach should be followed throughout the course and in examinations. There is always a reason for setting a question, and it will pay you to try to see what that reason is. Look at the wording of the subject you were given: were you asked to discuss (see different aspects of the topic and assess them), to analyse (work through critically, stage by stage), compare and contrast, give your own opinion or evaluation? The wording will give you an idea of what is wanted and, if you keep it in mind, you are far less likely to fall into the trap which is every lecturer's nightmare – writing all you know about the subject with no reference to what was asked for.

Writing or speaking in the context of student work has an in-built oddity: you are presenting information to someone who already knows, although the interpretation or analysis may well be your own. Keep this in mind, as it will affect what you write: you'll be expected to be reasonably thorough, using the information you have been given as a starting point, making use of a reading list to help you to read round the topic, assessing your material in a sensible and logical way, and giving your own critical opinion, backed up by quotation and example. Presumably you chose your subject because it interested you; show your interest by being prepared to give your own opinion, but make sure that it isn't a wild statement, unsubstantiated by evidence from your reading or the text in front of you.

As you write your first few pieces of work, there is a danger of over-explanation. Your lecturer knows the terms that are new to you and you don't need to define them, although an indication of your understanding is a good idea. Some information will be self-evident, and some will come directly from the lecture; some students will simply repeat what they have been told, and the result is uninspiring to mark. Try to find your own example rather than the one given in class, comment on something that you have seen, refer to a recent article on the subject, and the lecturer will be only too ready to give you extra credit.

So, you've arrived, gone through all the appropriate administrative channels, been to your first lecture, and now you have been given a piece of work to complete. It may seem very daunting, but remember that most students feel the same way and also that this is the beginning, and you wouldn't be there if you weren't willing to learn.

Key point: why have you been given a particular assignment? Look for clues about what's wanted.

▶ Writing and speaking

During your course, you'll have work to do which will involve you in both writing and speaking. Why should you have to do both and what are the differences?

Your time at college or university is an opportunity to develop yourself and your skills. It may seem to be a long way off, but eventually you will leave academic work and get a job, and the more skilled you are at both writing and speaking, the more successful you will be, whether you choose a career which directly involves writing, such as journalism, or one in which both writing and speaking to people are very important, such as personnel work. If you are a mature student, you may in your work already have used many of the forms of communication you meet again as a student, but you may be seeing them in a new light and perhaps examining them more critically than you have in the past. You may choose to change your career, or you may be looking for new professional opportunities.

But that's in the future: what you want from the next few years is a good qualification (apart from the enjoyment aspects, of course, which are themselves very important). You need to learn about your chosen subject, convey your knowledge and ask appropriate questions, and all these activities involve communication.

So what are the differences between writing and speaking? When you write an essay, dissertation or any similar work, you are setting out the knowledge you have gained, and your own response, in an accurate and formal way. As you prepare it, you can revise, correct or even delete your attempt and start again. The work you produce can be read and reread, studied, analysed and shared with other people. It may contain quotations, illustrations, reading lists or other specific information which helps the reader to see what you mean and follow it up. It may have a long life – if it's particularly good, your lecturer may keep a copy to show to other generations of students, long after you have finished your education.

Spoken communication, such as takes place in a seminar, discussion or formal presentation, is very different, by its very nature ephemeral and limited in scope. You may have to speak as part of a group; even then, you aren't likely to be speaking for more than twenty minutes or so, and when you've finished, the occasion has gone for ever. It's no good having a bright idea five minutes after the end of the session. (Your presentation may, of course, be recorded so that you can watch a video replay. This is helpful in improving your speaking skills, but it's almost certain that the video will be reused before long; your efforts are still short-lived.)

Think about one of your lectures, especially one which you found clear and interesting. It lasted perhaps fifty minutes, and you spent most of that time trying to get down as much information as possible in your notes, to the extent that you may hardly have been able to take in what you were told. A lecturer has advantages which aren't necessarily available to other speakers: he or she can come back to a point on the next occasion, refer you to an article or book for further detail, and even overrun by a few minutes if necessary, although this is not recommended. You are making notes and that will help you to remember. In spite of all this, it isn't easy to listen for fifty minutes and you may feel quite tired at the end. It's always difficult to absorb details just by listening – notice how little a good lecturer actually says in fifty minutes, and how little you could remember without your notes.

> *Key point: think through the advantages and disadvantages of writing and speaking: in your course, you'll be doing both.*

Writing and speaking are, then, quite different forms of communication, and you will be involved in both, at the receiving end through books and lectures, and at the giving end, by writing essays and leading discussions. In this book, we'll be giving you advice about all these. You'll soon appreciate that you can say and assimilate much less through speech than through writing, but that speech has an immediacy and energy that writing can't match. When you've just listened to a really good lecture, you will know exactly what we mean!

Part Two
Writing Skills

2 Listening, Reading and Making Notes

▶ Listening

Zeno of Citium, a wise ancient Greek, said that we have two ears and one mouth so that we might listen more and talk less. He did not – as far as we know – add that we need to be trained to do both. Obviously, we start by listening, and only by hearing people talking to us do we learn how to speak, copying the sounds we hear and eventually mastering a language. Later, given the inclination and some ability, we may listen to different people and so master another language: we may try to do this from a textbook, but we will not become fluent until we hear the words spoken in a natural context.

Listening is, then, essential to our development, but, as we said earlier of communication skills in general, most people aren't very good at listening. We assume that it is a natural skill and that we don't need to be taught it: in reality, we often hear, but don't necessarily bother to listen.

Within further and higher education, you are called upon to do a great deal of productive listening, in lectures, tutorials and seminars, in conversations with staff and other students, and sometimes from prerecorded material, a video for example. It's worth considering what helps us to listen effectively, and what are the barriers that cause us to lose concentration.

Barriers to listening
An obvious area of distraction is physical discomfort. If the seat we're sitting on is hard or gives us poor back support, we tend to fidget and be distracted; if the room is stuffy or the lighting poor, we find it difficult to concentrate. Background noise can be a nuisance, particularly if it's either loud and unpleasant (the lawn mower outside the window) or too attractive (someone playing one of our favourite pieces of music). We can also find

other people's conversations much more interesting than our own, especially if we hear our name mentioned – and it's interesting how we will
hear our own name through a great deal of other noise and in spite of
listening to something else. All these distractions may be outside our control, but if we take any opportunity to improve the situation (moving away
from the window if the sun is in our eyes), we will be helping ourselves to
listen more efficiently.

> *Key point: to listen effectively, try to avoid distractions such as physical
> discomfort and background noise.*

Speakers can themselves provide distraction, and it's worth considering
how they do this, not least to help us to avoid the same habits when we
ourselves are the speakers. If the voice is too soft or too fast to be heard
comfortably, we will simply stop making the effort (see pages 132–41 for
advice about good speaking). Mannerisms can distract: we've probably all
had the experience of remembering that the speaker took off and replaced
his or her spectacles twenty-five times; we recall this long after we've
forgotten the subject matter. A loud tie, ostentatious jewellery or totally
inappropriate footwear makes us look rather than listen; if there is
a clash between these two activities, looking nearly always wins. (One of us
can still remember, after many years, hearing an otherwise professional
presenter who, on a hot summer day, wore sandals and no socks, but
we've now no idea what he was talking about.)

Most of us, on occasion, suffer from a wandering mind. We can't help
noticing how pretty the flowers are outside the lecture room window,
and we start to daydream about our garden at home. We look forward,
instead of concentrating on the present, either to the near future, thinking
about our need for a cup of coffee after the lecture, or to the more distant
future, wondering whether we shall manage to get a better vacation job
than last year's, and then we start remembering how awful it was last
year, how hard we worked for so little money and so on. It's all too
easy and very human.

Positive listening
Can we remove these barriers to listening? The absolute answer is
probably no, but we can certainly listen more effectively than we often
manage to do. Part of the art of listening well is preparation. If we don't
know anything about the subject, or we don't know why we need to

listen to it, we imagine that it will be difficult to concentrate before we even start. Lecturers can help, of course, by telling us at the end of the previous week what they're going to talk about next time, and by starting the lecture with a quick summing up of the main ideas from last week's class and an introduction to what they are about to say, but sometimes we fail to listen to such help even when it's given. If we do listen, then we have the chance to read some background material, or at least to think beforehand what might be involved in the subject. We can ask ourselves why we need this information: perhaps because it's necessary background, because it's of general interest, or in order to be able to write about it in the examination. If we have some idea of the topic and the purpose of the lecture, we are far more likely to be able to concentrate.

> *Key point: prepare to listen. Decide why you need the information and why it's important to you.*

We are also helped by taking notes. We'll discuss various forms of notes later in this chapter (see pages 25–35), but apart from any other considerations, taking notes helps us to concentrate. We have to listen in order to know what to write. Of course we may occasionally go onto automatic pilot and write without really thinking, but it's hard to concentrate on one thing while you're writing about a different topic, and the physical exercise involved in writing tends to keep our minds active in the right direction.

There are other more dangerous distractions which may afflict you, such as lack of interest. Some parts of most courses will be highly congenial, and other parts less so, but if you're going to do well in the examinations, you can't afford to switch off; in any case, you may find that the topic is more interesting than you expected if you listen carefully. As human beings, we are good at not hearing what we don't want to hear, and if we've decided in advance that the subject is boring and useless, then our minds are predisposed to find something more interesting to think about.

As a student, you can also try to be more active in class. Asking questions is an obvious way to increase your interest and therefore your attention, but as listeners, we can also give helpful signals to the lecturer. When we are talking, we know how important the audience's response is (see pages 145–6 for a discussion of this point); if we lean forward, respond to eye contact, nod when we agree or look questioning if we're puzzled, an experienced lecturer will pick up the signals and respond to them.

There will be pauses in the lecture, often to allow students to catch up with the note-taking. Use this gap to think about the notes you're writing; try quickly to summarize the argument or foresee what is coming next. As you become more involved, you will find it easier to concentrate.

A clash of personalities nearly always makes communication more difficult. If you are listening to a lecturer you dislike for some reason, or who you suspect dislikes you, you will instinctively not want to listen or respond. It's worth sitting down and thinking quietly about the situation, away from class. Have you a genuine grievance against the lecturer? If so, you need to talk to someone, perhaps your tutor, about it; however, such discussion is outside the scope of this book. Is it something about the actual lecture which you're finding difficult? If so, do other people have the same problem? If they do, then it might be worth going as a small group to ask the lecturer to speak more slowly or give more help or whatever the problem is. If it's simply a matter of a clash of personality or, as sometimes happens, a dislike originating with someone else, the only answer is to respond in a professional way: it's a pity that this is happening, but it isn't the fault of the subject and it certainly isn't going to result in you getting a poor result in your exams; you will therefore do your best to listen attentively. This may be an occasion for enlisting the help of a friend in the class and discussing this aspect of the work together; this can be a useful way of generating interest.

It's possible to be too personally involved with the subject for easy listening. We can jump ahead ('I know what's coming next and so I don't need to listen') or, more dangerously, we may prejudge the issue. We may have such strong opinions on the matter that we simply don't want to hear anybody else's theory. This is a highly unacademic attitude: if we want to study the subject in depth, we must be ready to hear all sides of the problem, and only then to make up our own minds. If we're too emotionally involved with what is said, we may spend the time planning our own response ('just wait till I can say what I think') rather than giving due consideration to the point of view being expressed.

Ideally, we concentrate on the speaker, reserving our judgement about the subject and making careful notes (see pages 26–8). It isn't just a question of hearing and recording the words; we learn also from the speaker's tone of voice and the non-verbal communication employed (see also pages 141–5). Lecturers may put forward a point of view in the hope that we will recognize its weakness; they may put forward a theory with which they themselves profoundly disagree; they themselves, being human, will have prejudices and may give us a partial or subjective point of view. If we are both listening and noticing the tone of voice used, we can often pick up such feelings and they will guide us in our response. As students, you are not expected to agree with everything you are told, but you need a sound basis for your disagreement. Careful and critical listening is the first step. As the philosopher A N Whitehead said, 'A clash of doctrines is not a disaster – it is an opportunity.'

> *Key point: take notes, ask questions and listen critically. Be involved.*

▶ Reading lists

You will probably not have spent long in further or higher education before you are given a reading list. It may look daunting; it may contain more material than you have ever had to read before. Don't panic. You aren't necessarily expected to read everything on the list: there may well be alternatives listed, for the very practical reason that there are far more students studying the course than copies of the relevant books in the library.

Our advice is, of course, only general. Individual lecturers devise their own booklists in different ways, and you need to read your list carefully for clues about the relevance of various titles. Nevertheless, it's worth noting that every book on a booklist is not of equal importance to every other book.

Enjoy your reading. You have a wonderful, but limited, opportunity to read about the subject you have chosen to study; almost certainly, it's the only such chance you will ever get. The more you read, the more you will become involved with your work and the more satisfying it may well become. However, there are different ways to read, and it's essential to know how to vary your reading pattern.

> *Key point: tackle reading lists in a positive way, and enjoy your reading.*

▶ Reading skills

People read in different ways and at different speeds. Interestingly, the first research on eye movements in reading was carried out in France as long ago as the late nineteenth century. It was discovered that people's eyes don't move smoothly from left to right when they are reading; they move in a jerky way, 'fixating' on words for a fraction of a second. Some readers 'fixate' frequently, often rereading words, while others seem to take in a whole line of print while 'fixating' only two or three times. This is one of the major differences between fast and slow readers.

This book does not include a rapid reading course. Such courses exist and can be helpful. However, there are various ways in which you can be guided to read more efficiently, which is very useful when you have so much to get through. You may also find that you can read rather more quickly than you expected, partly with practice and partly because you have to a certain extent planned how you are going to read each piece of writing.

If you never become a fast reader, don't worry. There is no correlation between rapid reading and intelligence: some highly intelligent people are slow readers. The only problem is that if you read very slowly, you may lose an oversight of the whole passage; if you try to read a bit more quickly, you may concentrate more fully and so remember more of what you read.

Preparing to read

Reading is a physical as well as a mental activity, and your physical wellbeing is therefore important to the efficiency of your reading. You'll remember how reasonable comfort helps you to listen and how discomfort distracts; it's the same with reading. Sit with the book at the right height for you, whether you're holding it or putting it on your desk or table. Most important of all, check that you have a good directed light – try not to sit so that the book is in your own shadow. If you have difficulty reading at the same distance as your friends, go to an optician and make sure that if you need spectacles, you have them.

Before you start to read, ask yourself some questions:

- What information are you hoping to get from this book (article or whatever)?
- Why do you want this information?
- What do you already know about the subject, and so at what level do you need the information?
- Are you going to read for general interest, or because you need to memorize the contents?

We don't always read for the same purpose or, therefore, in the same way. You may be looking for just one piece of information, and the rest of the book is of no interest: you therefore scan the pages in order to find what you want. You may want to check your own knowledge, and so you skim the pages, stopping only if you find a problem. You might be evaluating the book to see if it's worth reading, in which case you will probably dip into it here and there, spending more time on the contents page than on any other. If you need to learn the information for an exam, you will read more slowly, concentrating on each idea and maybe rereading extensively. The extreme of slow, intensive reading is perhaps checking proofs, when you are concentrating on each word, perhaps each letter, and we know from experience that in so doing, you tend to lose track of the message; it's possible to proof-read a book and have only a vague idea of the content at the end!

So your reason for reading is very important, as it will affect the way in which you approach the task, and therefore your success or failure. It's very easy to waste time by choosing the wrong method of reading: we all know the problem of skimming a book to evaluate it and finding that the material is irrelevant to our needs but absolutely fascinating, so that we're still reading the same book half an hour later! This is most enjoyable, of course, but not recommended if we're in a hurry.

> *Key point: practise a variety of reading styles, and choose the right one for your immediate purpose.*

Reading critically

We have to decide what not to read. There is a tendency, often among bright, interested students, to try to read too much. Booklists need to be approached critically; we need also to have the courage to discard material because it isn't really what we need at the time. Of course we may go on reading out of interest, but if we have an assignment and limited time, it may be more sensible to make a note of what we'd like to read and go back to it later. We may discard material because it's at the wrong level: there's always a temptation to read what we already know because it makes us feel good, but such reading may not be productive. If we find that the book is at too advanced a level, we perhaps ought to discard it or note it for the future and then leave it, because if we don't, we may become confused or disheartened.

We also need to allow thinking time. It's good that we spend time in reading widely before we write an essay, but if we don't have a chance to sit back and consider what we've read, to assimilate it, be critical and maybe come up with a new idea of our own, then what we write will be secondhand, worthy, perhaps, but with little individuality. This thinking time also helps us to remember what we've read, as we're allowing it to become our own property, rather than just words on a page.

There is a temptation to believe what we see in print. This is very natural, and in that a book has been through a selection process by a publisher, it has some credibility; however, this cannot be relied on without question. Take the example of two newspapers of different political persuasions, published on the same day and recording the same events. Each has been selective, as they consider different happenings to be important or controversial. They may have different formats, which draw attention to (or hide) particular information; one may have pictures to make a story more graphic while the other uses the bottom corner of the left-hand page to make the same story less noticeable. The words will be different: the English language has a great many words which say more or less the same thing with different emphasis, and so one paper may find a story 'sensational' while the other finds it 'intriguing'; one may describe a particular politician as 'frank' or 'outspoken' while the other describes the same person as 'tactless' or even 'devious'.

This is an extreme example, of course; textbooks are unlikely to indulge in such rhetoric. Nevertheless, a book may be written in defence of a particular point of view, in order to attack a different approach or because of a passionate conviction on the part of the writer. A philosophical subject such as euthanasia or genetic engineering, for example, can be treated in very different ways, and 'facts' can be produced to prove almost anything. If a book seems to have been written from one strongly held point of view, it's worth trying a book or an article on the same subject by someone else, to see if the message is different. Check the date to see if more modern scholarship has overtaken what used to be an accepted viewpoint. Your lecturers may help in this by mentioning that a particular writer has a notable prejudice; information you were given in class might undermine the argument. Ask questions from your own general knowledge, and note whether the book gives you an answer. If not, can you guess why not? Reading critically makes the whole task more enjoyable.

> *Key point: be aware of an author's point of view, and try to read, or think of, the opposing arguments.*

Realistic reading

If you are reading a thriller on holiday, you may become so involved with the story that you read the whole book at one sitting. You will have forgotten most of it within a day or two, but that won't matter. If, however, you are reading material which you need to remember for examination purposes, you cannot afford to read in this way. Again, you must adapt your method of reading to your circumstances.

It would be unrealistic to try to read the whole of a textbook as you read the thriller. Concentration is short-lived, and you need to use this fact to help you to read productively. Set yourself realistic targets – finishing a chapter or a section, or perhaps just reading a few pages. Stop when you have completed this and take stock. Try to summarize what you have read; make notes on it, perhaps using more than one form of notes (see pages 31–2). Ask yourself one or two questions on the basis of what you have read, to check your understanding and your memory. If the material is difficult, and you find it hard to concentrate sufficiently, bribe yourself with the promise of a cup of tea or coffee at the end of the chapter. A few minutes' break will in any case help to keep you going. When you feel that you have completed enough work for the day, be willing to forget about it for the time being and go out to meet your friends. Next day, start by trying to recall the essentials of what you read the previous day; you will then be more likely to go on working with the positive attitude which will help you to remember.

> *Key point: read critically, with realistic criteria and sensible breaks.*

Choosing and using books

There's a shape to almost everything you write: an essay has a beginning, middle and end (no surprise) and a dissertation has chapters, starting with an introduction and developing the information in a logical way until the overall assessment of the evidence, probably called the conclusion. This is much like the shape of a book, and it's a useful guide to whether a particular work is worth skimming through, reading with care or even buying. You will handle far more books than you could possibly read during your course, and it's useful to have a checklist which helps you to decide a book's category and, even more important, to avoid mistakes which are expensive in both time and money.

Assessing a book

- *Title*: the title of a book indicates its subject matter; it may also give a pointer towards its approach or level – 'an introduction', for instance.

- *Date*: the date when the book was published is very important; opinions and fashions change, and you need to know if the ideas are current or long since superseded.

- *Preface*: this will probably tell you more about the author, including other books which he or she has written. Note whether any of them is familiar, through a comment by your lecturer, a review or your own reading. You may also learn about the author's prejudices, and about the level at which the book is written.

- *Contents*: this is extremely important, and much of your scanning of a book will start here, whether you are looking for specific information or checking the coverage of the subject. Sometimes there is a useful short summary after the title of each chapter.

- *Introduction*: it's worth reading quickly through this, as it will give you a clearer picture of the author's purpose and the level at which the book is written. It will also indicate what is not covered in the book.

- *Chapters*: chapters have their own titles. These help you to find your way round the book and read it selectively. They give you a useful overview of the content, and may also convey a sense of logical progression through the material.

- *Individual pages*: using the index (see below), find a page which discusses a topic you are interested in. Skim read this page, glancing at the beginning of each paragraph and allowing your eye to pick out key words or phrases. If you decide to read the book, you will be at the mercy of the writer, and it's helpful to check if the style is encouraging. If it's written in a dense, clumsy or patronising style, you may want to think twice before committing yourself (especially to buying such a book).

- *Illustrations*: these often show you the level of the book and its quality; they can be a quick and attractive way of conveying information.

- *Index*: many textbooks have an index, to enable you to find specific details quickly and easily. It's also useful in helping you to decide whether the information is appropriate for your purposes: look up two or three topics and see how much detail is given for each. Follow up one or two cross-references, which will show you more about the way in which the material has been organized.

- *Publisher's blurb*: there will probably be a short piece of writing on the back cover which tells you something about the book, its intended readership and the author. This can be useful, but remember that its primary purpose is to entice you to buy!

Key point: use this checklist to assess books in the library or the bookshop.

Remembering what you read

Sadly, we all forget most of what we read. We are overloaded with information, nowadays on the Internet as well as in printed form, and our brains find it difficult to cope. If we are to remember what we read for examination purposes, we must employ techniques to help us to remember. Notes, which are discussed in more detail below, are the most useful technique, as the physical action of writing encourages us to remember, and in any case we have the notes themselves to go back to.

If you find a book in the library or on a friend's bookshelf, you can't, of course, make notes in it. You may want to make your own written notes in the usual way, but if there are a few pages of special interest, it's worth photocopying them and then marking them up (see page 27) for yourself. (The law of copyright allows you to make one copy for your personal use.) Above all, make sure that you record enough about the book to be able to find it again later (again, see the section on taking notes, page 28).

Your friends are especially useful in helping to fix information in your mind. They are probably in two categories: those who are studying the same subjects, and those who aren't. Both are useful. Meet your class colleagues regularly, in small groups, and revise together, or discuss a particular lecture, or a book which you have all read. You may get a different perspective on the material, the discussion may itself be a pleasant experience and you are confirming what you have read. If you hear a different and interesting piece of information, make a note of it as soon as you can, at an appropriate place in your notes.

Friends who are studying another subject can also be persuaded, perhaps on an exchange basis, to listen as you describe a topic which you are studying. They have no preconceptions and are therefore more likely to see inconsistencies or an illogical argument. Sometimes an apparently 'simple' question from them can make you look at a topic in a new light or clarify your thinking. You are then likely to remember the context.

There are techniques for helping you to remember specific facts – you may have met some of these at school or in your previous work. If you have, then don't hesitate to use them again. It doesn't matter if they seem rather silly, in fact, in some ways the sillier they are, the better. You may, for example, relate a difficult fact to an ordinary, everyday object; if you associate your fact with the kettle, then you will find that when you pick up the kettle to make coffee in the morning, the fact comes unbidden into your mind. Association is a useful way of helping us to remember what we read, which is why using a pattern or colour in notes (see page 31) is such a good idea – it's easier to remember a pattern than a great many words.

> *Key point: find helpful ways of memorizing information, for example by discussion or word association.*

Reading practice

As with most skills, reading improves with regular practice. Try to make a daily routine for yourself of a certain amount of reading connected with your course. Apart from anything else, this will help you to keep your work up to date and be prepared for future lectures. Don't limit yourself to this: read other material regularly, such as a newspaper or a magazine connected with one of your hobbies. As you read these things, practise varying the way you read. Skim some passages, summarize others as you finish them, try to read more quickly by allowing your eyes to 'fixate' on only two or three key words in a line, taking in the other words through your peripheral vision, and refusing to go back if you feel that you've missed something. You will find that your general reading speed becomes a little quicker, and that you are more adept at varying the way in which you read. Be willing to slow right down to perhaps only a hundred words a minute, or even fewer, if what you are reading is complex, and to speed up to at least four hundred words a minute if you are familiar with what you are reading.

> *Key point: practise reading in different ways and at different speeds, so that your reading skills improve.*

Read critically, not only to assess the usefulness of what you have read, but also to improve your own writing style. If you find a passage or an article particularly easy, try to analyse why this is so, and what features of the writer's style have helped you. Extend your vocabulary by finding new words in what you read, and enjoy the challenge of trying to write more fluently yourself. Efficient reading and a good writing style are advantages which last a lifetime.

▶ Making notes

While you are a student, much of your time is taken up with making notes, from lectures and seminars, books and journals, CD-ROMs and the Internet. You will probably find that your lecturers take it for granted that you are competent at this skill; if you have had no help in the past, you may find it difficult at first.

This section will consider making notes from these different sources and will give an example of how this might be done in practice. Of course, the application of these techniques will depend to some extent on your subject, and you may need to adapt the suggestions as appropriate. However, we can give you some guidelines which will generally be of use.

Know why you are taking notes before you start. You will have seen that we've made more or less the same point about starting to listen and to read: there is a great deal of emphasis throughout this book on the need to prepare thoroughly before undertaking almost any student activity. Much time is wasted by lack of preparation, and if you don't think about your motivation for taking notes, as with other aspects of your course, you will find that they are less helpful than you expected.

We make notes primarily to help us to remember, but some notes are for immediate or short-term use, and others for use in the long term. Clarify your purpose: if you need notes just for a specific assignment, you may make them in an abbreviated form with indifferent handwriting, as you will be able to remember enough to make everything sufficiently clear. If you are going to need your notes for exams in several months' time, you must be much more careful that everything is clearly written and all abbreviations explained. It's all too easy to be sure that you would never forget... until you see your notes again a year later.

Your notes may be intended as general background reading, in which case they may be much less detailed than those which must be memorized. Lecture notes are likely to be reasonably full, but should not include witty asides or jokes made by the lecturer in order to give the occasion a little light relief (although if the wit helps you to remember, there is a case for noting it, but not for repeating it in an exam paper).

> *Key point: decide on your objectives before you start, especially whether your notes are for short-term or long-term use.*

Notes from lectures

Lecturers use a range of techniques, and you will soon become familiar with your lecturers' idiosyncrasies. You will also soon identify good and less good lecturers; remember to take action if your group has real difficulties in a specific case. If the subject is new to you, you may wish to consider buying an introductory book of the 'Made Simple' type, in order to give you some background and help with unfamiliar terms.

Sometimes, the lecturer gives you a clue about what is to follow, by saying 'There are two aspects to this', or 'I'm going to suggest four different approaches'. Number your notes – it will help to fix the information in your mind. A good lecturer will also provide headings, by making it clear when a new aspect of the subject is about to begin or when a different point of view follows. The format you are creating will be very useful to you when you revise from your notes. When you look at the page again in six months' time, the headings and the lists will stand out and refresh your memory.

All notes, from any source, must be dated. As we've already indicated, information can go out of date and it may be of great importance that you remember that you made your notes before a particularly controversial article was published, for instance. Within each lecture, number your pages. The combination of date and page number will help you to keep all your notes in the correct order, which may be particularly important if, for example, you take out a few pages to lend to a friend who was ill and missed the lecture. If you do this, incidentally, always make sure that you agree when the notes are to be returned and check that they are – you will need your own notes for revision purposes.

Some lecturers give handout material to their students. There are two advantages to this: you can concentrate on listening to the lecture as you will need to write less, and you can be reasonably sure that the information on the handout is accurate (and legible). The disadvantage is that it is easy to assume that because we have a handout, we know the information on it, even without reading it. If we are to remember, we must make the handout our own, by marking it up after the lecture and adding comments from our own reading. It should also be dated and numbered along with our own notes.

As we said earlier, human beings are not, for the most part, good listeners. Don't assume that because something is clear in the lecture, or in your notes, that you will necessarily still understand it months later. For this reason, it is a good idea to go through your notes as soon as possible after the lecture, on the same day if this can be done. If you find a gap in your understanding, talk the problem over with colleagues or ask the lecturer at the next class. Add headings and number lists where you can. Underline or highlight points which you must especially remember. Rewrite your notes in a different format (this is also a good way of revising them). Colour-code each page, perhaps highlighting in red the points which are important and in blue the points which you want to look up later. You need to be able to remember this information later, and the colour pattern on the page will help you to visualize the content.

Nowadays, students sometimes wish to record their notes without the need to scribble frantically with pen and paper. If you would like to use a cassette recorder for the lecture, or if you need to do so because of a disability, courtesy demands that you ask the lecturer's permission first. It is unlikely to be refused. Recording the lecture has the disadvantage that you don't immediately have notes to mark up or revise from later, and a recording can easily be wiped out by mistake (for this reason, it's a good idea to summarize your notes as soon as possible after the class); you will also depend upon the lecturer's voice; if you try to record a lecturer who is given to walking around the room, you may have only a partial record of what was said.

Laptop computers are sometimes used for taking notes, and they have the advantage – provided the user can type quickly and accurately enough – of producing clear, legible notes. The two provisos are important, though, and if the note-taker gets tired or left behind, the record is not as helpful as it should be. Before you use any aid such as a cassette recorder or a computer, check the room to make sure that there is a power point nearby if you need it, and that the battery isn't going to run out before the end. Whatever equipment you use, notes should be printed out and marked up as soon as possible after the class.

> *Key point: when you're making notes from a lecture, record useful information and mark it up as soon as possible after the class.*

▶ Recording information from printed sources

Much of your note-taking will be from books, journals and other published material, and it is essential that you record as many details of your sources as possible. There is an obvious practical reason for this, in that you may well need to go back to the information later to check it or for further details. It's enormously frustrating to know what the book you used looks like but to have forgotten the author's name.

There is an even more important reason for recording the published material you use. A book or article is the result of someone's thinking and experience, often of their research, and it remains their 'intellectual property'. If this material is used without credit being given to the writer, the property is in effect stolen, and this is as serious an offence as any other theft, especially in an academic community in which people's careers depend to a certain extent on their publications.

> *Key point: record important bibliographical information so that you can reference it accurately.*

As a result of all this, you will need to indicate the fact clearly when you use material published by someone else. You may quote exactly, in which case you need to show the extent of the quotation: if it is a few words only, put them in quotation marks (normally single quote marks); if you quote more than one line of print, introduce your quotation with a colon, start it on a new line and indent that line and any subsequent lines of quotation, so that the block of text stands out clearly from the rest of your writing. In this case, there are of course no quotation marks.

There are different conventions for setting out the information which you put at the end of your assignment or dissertation, and your lecturer may give you guidelines. One of the two most commonly used ways of identifying a quotation in the text is by using superscript arabic numbers in sequence. (Superscript numbers, if you haven't come across them before, are little numbers raised above the line of print). The other system involves using the author's surname, date of publication and page reference in brackets (this is known as the Harvard system). This latter form has the advantage that your lecturer will probably recognize the reference from the information on the page and may not need to look it up. However, you may be told to use one system or the other, or a modified version of either, or to follow the advice given in the latest edition of the Modern Humanities Research Association (MHRA) *Style Book*, which is widely used, although often in a simplified form, by humanities departments. As we said above, but it's worth repeating, you must check the exact form of references with your department.

> *Key point: check the form of references required by your department and use it consistently.*

In both forms of reference, you need to give all the relevant bibliographical information at the end of your essay or dissertation. The first example that follows could have as its textual mark either a superscript number, or, if you are following the Harvard system, (Peck and Coyle, 2002, p46). At the end of your text, you would give the full details in the order appropriate to the system you are using, as follows:

(after a superscript number)
John Peck and Martin Coyle, *Literary Terms and Criticism*, 3rd edn (Basingstoke: Palgrave Macmillan, 2002).

(using the Harvard system)
Peck, John and Coyle, Martin, 2002, *Literary Terms and Criticism*, 3rd edn, Basingstoke, Palgrave Macmillan.

You will see that the publisher's name and place of publication are included. The edition number is also given unless the book is the first edition: this is important, as the page numbering might be different in different editions. The date is important, as it shows whether you are using material published a long time ago or more recently.

Note that when there are two authors, both are named, but if there are more than two, use the first named and then *et al* ('and others'). There are various other Latin tags which can be used as you make up your list of references, such as *ibid* (the reference is to the same work as the previous reference) and *op cit* (the work has been referenced earlier), but unless you are confident in using them, they are generally better avoided.

A moment ago, we mentioned using published work without actually quoting from it. You may want to refer to someone's research, for instance, without actually quoting the words of the original article. You are still using someone else's intellectual property, and it is essential that you show that you are doing so. The format is the same: when you have referred to the research, use a superscript number or the Harvard system in exactly the way in which you would show a quotation, and again put all the details at the end.

There is a grey area in using references, and it can lead students into trouble. Some information which was originally the result of someone's research is now so well known that it can be said to be 'in the public domain'. The reference earlier to the research into eye movements in reading is in this category: most educated people know that a reader 'fixates' on particular words several times in a line of print; the fact has been used in print so often that there is now no need to give a specific reference. You will often see from your own general knowledge that particular information is in this category, but if you are in doubt, either ask your lecturer or give a reference anyway.

Using intellectual property which is not your own without referring to your source (Plagiarism) is very serious, and every student should be aware of the dangers of doing so. For this reason, you are strongly advised to put into your own notes immediately all the details of any material which you take from a published source. At the time, you will be aware that the material is not your own, but there is a risk that in a year's time you could copy it directly into your essay or dissertation and forget that it wasn't yours originally. It is an easy mistake to make, but the consequences could be disastrous, for it would be very difficult to prove that you had no intention of stealing someone else's words. Develop the habit of noting your sources every time you gather information, so that there is no danger of your facing this problem. It will also then be easy for you to build up your list of references at the end of your assignment.

▶ Formats for notes

As you make notes from books and articles, try to use headings and numbers in the way that we suggested for your lecture notes (see page 27). You have more time at the stage of actually writing the notes than when you revise from them, and if you make them look clear and interesting by colour-coding, you will find this helpful when you use them again later.

You are probably used to making notes on sheets of A4 paper used in the portrait position. There are other possibilities, which you may want to use when you are revising for exams. You will be going through pages of notes, taken from lectures and published sources perhaps over several months or even years. The notes will sometimes look heavy and uninspiring, and you may feel an understandable reluctance to spend time reading them over and over again. We have already suggested using colour to add interest and as an aid to your memory; you may also find it helpful to produce new notes in a different form. Summarize each page of your notes in a sentence or two, highlighting the most important facts; summarize several pages in a paragraph, again emphasizing what matters most. You will find that the task of producing the summary itself helps you to remember, and the summaries will be invaluable for last-minute revision.

> Key point: vary the form of your notes, using patterns, highlighting and colour to help you to revise efficiently.

Your notes could also be reproduced in a more visually attractive way, as a 'spider diagram'. Turn a large sheet of paper on its side, into landscape position, and then write your main topic in the centre of the sheet. Now add subordinate information around the 'spider body', very briefly, preferably only two or three words at a time. Draw a circle around each piece of information. Now try to group the circles, either by drawing lines or using different colours to make associations between various points which may have appeared in different areas of the page. You may also be able to add subordinate circles to your main circles, to show when a major point has perhaps two or three lesser facts associated with it. After a little while, you will find that you have a structure to your notes, and, if you feel it would be helpful, you might want to redraw the spider, now making all the connections clear.

It takes a bit of practice before you can draw a spider diagram quickly and easily, but if you try it out a few times, you will find that you can rewrite and organize your notes at speed. You will also have a great deal of material recorded in a small space, and if you draw the spider on a large file card, you can carry material for revision round in your pocket: each time you look at the spider, the circles will jog your memory about important facts which you need to remember. As you will see (page 40), we recommend this method of organizing material for essays, dissertations and indeed almost all you write, and your presentations, too.

It is easier to see this process than to read about it and so we've given below, in Figure 2.1, some of the information from the start of this chapter as a spider diagram. Later in the book (see pages 42,43), we've given a further example of the use of a spider diagram in organizing material. It will help you to produce a set of headings when you need them, for example in a report or a dissertation, or when you need a structure without actually showing the headings, as in an essay. Try it out for yourself, starting with information which is fairly straightforward, and you will probably soon be able to produce notes and organize your material in this way without difficulty.

▶ Notes from the Internet and similar sources

Nowadays, students are expected to take notes from computer sources as well as the more traditional books and journals. There are, as with any other material, good and bad aspects to this: somewhere on the Internet, for example, there is probably most of the information you need; there is also a vast amount of other material, so that it can take a long time to find exactly what you want.

The scale of the problem is immense. One hour is 3600 seconds. If you can call up and scan a page in 20 seconds (which is quite speedy), in one hour you can see 180 pages. If you carry out a search and find a thousand references, it will take at least 10 hours to look at them all briefly, and this doesn't include either the time taken to make notes or pauses while you have something to eat.

Before you start on such an enormous task, therefore, it's wise to find the addresses of suitable sites from lecturers, colleagues or journals. There is another reason for this: there is currently very little control over what appears on the Internet, less than might be expected from a refereed journal or reputable publisher. If you have any reason to doubt the

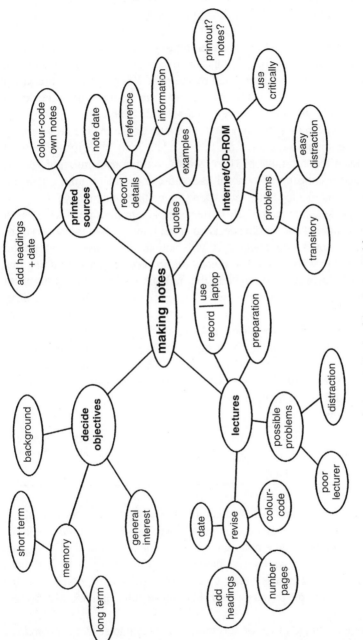

Figure 2.1 *Making notes spider*

accuracy of the information you find (accepting that the website of a known and respected organization is likely to be reliable), take notes and cross-check them with other sources that you can trust.

Information on the Internet is temporary. This is an advantage, in that you can reasonably expect that it is up to date, but it's also a disadvantage, in that it may have disappeared by the next day, or even sooner. If you find something useful, either print it out or make notes from the screen immediately, as you may never get a second chance.

The decision whether to print out for later use or make notes from the screen is largely a matter of the time available and the purpose for which you need the information. There is also a cost consideration: if you are charged for the time, it is almost certainly worth printing out useful screens and making notes later. Don't spend time and money printing out more pages than you're likely to need; read them through quickly on the screen and make a sensible decision about how much of the material you are really going to find helpful. Always note the reference on your printed page and in your notes. There is as yet no accepted form for doing this, but make sure that you include the author's name and the title of the article, the website reference (www. followed by the name) and the date.

Just because the contents of the Internet are so vast, there is an even greater temptation to be distracted than there is in a bookshop or library. You are almost certain to catch sight of information which seems much more attractive than the subject you're researching. Make a note of it, and then return to the subject which is your priority; you can go back to other topics when time, or money, permit.

Key point: when you make notes from the Internet, be selective, print out if appropriate and record the source and date. Try not to be distracted by irrelevant information.

Note-taking from CD-ROMs is more like using books and journals, in that the information is more or less permanent and easily searched. The source and date of the material will be on the label and should be used in your references, with the addition of [on CD-ROM]. Again, you will need to decide whether it is better to save time by making notes from the screen, or print the pages out and either make notes or mark up the pages later.

There is a huge range of information available to students nowadays; much of it is very up to date, especially that which comes by way of the computer. A book is nearly always at least a year, and a journal may be even more, out of date because of the time taken by the process of publication, but a reputable textbook carries a weight of expertise which you can use again and again. All this material is potentially available to every student in your class and it would be foolish to ignore such rich sources of knowledge. Your job is to be selective, and then to make the information you find usable by organizing and assimilating it, often in discussion with your fellow students; it becomes your tool, but the job will be finished by your own critical thought processes.

3 Essays, Reports and Dissertations

In the previous chapter, we've looked at reading and making notes; in Chapter 4, we'll look at writing styles. In the following pages, we'll discuss the types of assignment you are likely to be given and the skills you will need to complete them successfully. You may meet any or all three of the following during your student career:

- *Essays*: you will already be familiar with essay writing from school, and the essay will continue to be the most frequent assignment you are given, both during your course and in your exams; you may also have to write 'long essays' and so we've briefly discussed those, too
- *Reports*: you may not have come across reports before, unless you've met them at work, and they are still comparatively rare in your type of course; nevertheless, we've included some guidance so that you can recognize a report if you meet one and can prepare one if you're asked to do so
- *Dissertations*: towards the end of your study, and in your postgraduate course if you do one, you are likely to write an extended dissertation; this requires detailed preparation and a good deal of writing, and so we have looked at the main requirements and techniques involved in fulfilling them.

▶ Essays

Surprisingly, essay writing causes new students a great deal of anxiety. You have written essays in your school and public exams for several years, but you are probably unsure about the requirements of an essay in further or higher education. You may also receive much less guidance than you've been used to: a lecture or two and a reading list. If you're a mature student, you may remember writing essays at school, but feel that they are a long way in the past and you can't remember how to start. Where do you go from there?

Perhaps the most important realization is that almost all students feel the same way about the first essay or two they write. Essays are important, in that they are a way for your lecturers to see how much you have understood and how sensibly you are tackling the course; they may also count towards your final result, depending on how strong an emphasis your department puts on continuous assessment. In Chapter 8, we look at forms of assessment, and consider essay writing there, too. The most immediate function of essays, however, is entirely for your benefit: they allow you to use, and so develop, the skills of selection, organization and good writing which are some of the most precious assets you can have, in almost every area of your future life.

> *Key point: essay writing helps you to develop the skills of selection, organization and good writing.*

So approach essay writing in a positive frame of mind and don't put it off so that the whole exercise is pushed into the last hour or two before the essay is due in. If you do, you will find it difficult to read sufficiently widely and, just as importantly, you won't have time for thinking, planning and checking, which are stages of almost as much value as the actual writing.

Answering the question

How do you start? You've been given a topic, so start by looking at the exact wording of the question. Essays can be of different types, and you need to be sure which approach is right for the one you are going to tackle. Some essays call for description rather than anything else, and these are easy to recognize because the question nearly always starts with 'Describe...'. These are rare at your level of work. Far more commonly, essay subjects put forward a proposition, and you are invited to assess it in the light of evidence and your own response. Such essays often have a sentence followed by the word 'Discuss'. Variants on this are a quotation followed by 'Discuss this comment with reference to ...', 'What evidence do you find for this view of ...?', 'How far would you agree ...?' and 'To what extent is it true to say that ...?'

We're already seeing different approaches to the subject. Pure description, as we've said, is unlikely, so make sure that you don't respond to a 'discuss' essay by just describing. If you are asked to discuss an aspect of Shakespeare's comedies, don't simply have a paragraph or two for each comedy in turn, finishing with it and then moving on to the next, showing each time how the aspect is revealed. Think how, when or why the aspect can be seen and group your examples so that you are discussing how Shakespeare reveals (or fails to reveal) the aspect, rather than just giving instances.

If the essay asks you to 'discuss with reference to' a particular text or theory, or a specific historical incident, then do just that. Don't feel that if you know more about another text or another historical incident, it's all right to say a little bit about the one you were asked for and then move on to the one you really wanted to discuss. It isn't. Make sure that you focus on exactly what you were asked for, with perhaps a passing reference to other examples. (This is, of course, a trap in exams, which we'll come back to in Chapter 8.)

There's also the 'What evidence do you find…?' type of essay. Obviously, you will look at the appropriate material and find evidence to quote. Remember that there's always the conflicting view – evidence *against* the proposition – and you need to look for that and include it too. Assess the evidence for and against, remembering that your essay needs to present a balanced view, even though you may decide that the evidence for or against is overwhelming. We'll say more about this when we give an example of an essay outline on pages 40–6.

You may also meet 'Compare and contrast' essays. Make sure that you give an appropriate weight to both comparison and contrast, and to each of the pieces of evidence you have been asked to discuss; it's easy to be swayed by your own like or dislike and forget the balance you were asked for.

There's one other aspect of this type of essay, and although it's simply a question of being careful and checking what you're doing, it's something that goes wrong far too often. You may be asked to 'Discuss one of the following (themes, poems, ideas or similar) with reference to two (pieces of evidence, events, novels or similar).' It seems easy, but halfway through, you could be sidetracked into writing about two of the following…, or using more pieces of evidence or more novels than you were told to. Check at regular intervals that you are still within the terms of the essay title you were given.

A slightly different type of question is the 'analysis' essay, which probably starts with something like 'Analyse the causes of… '. This has much in common with the 'discuss' question, but the word 'analyse' suggests that you are assessing the weight of pieces of evidence by grouping and comparing them. Remember that there are many different types of cause, for instance social, historical, religious or personal, and that what you are examining may have a mixture of any or all of these. Causes can also be long term, short term or immediate, as the causes of the First World War included rivalry in the Empire, naval build-up and its repercussions and the shooting of the Archduke Ferdinand in Sarajevo. You may need to decide which causes were most important: there might be many necessary causes but only one sufficient cause. This is part of your analysis.

You've no doubt been told many times to 'answer the question' and, to do this well, you need to be sure what the question is asking for, at this level of study as at any other. Check the exact wording: are you discussing what did happen, what might happen if, what should happen? It's useful to make a few notes before you start, jotting down what the question means, in terms of 'I must look at both', 'is there an argument against?', 'I must choose one theme – which?' 'I must look for causes over a long historical period as well as just before the event', and so on. Check back from time to time, during your preparatory reading and during the writing, to make sure that you are still in line with your own notes.

> Key point: decide what type of question you've been given, and answer the same question.

You may be given a word length for your essay and this is useful, as it guides you to the amount of information required. Check with your departmental handbook to see whether the word limit includes or excludes quotations, as they might have a serious impact on the number of words you have available.

Structuring your essay

Your first structuring activity might start early in the preparation process, in other words, as you think about the question and its implications. As you read and make notes, and decide how you are going to tackle the subject, ideas will be coming into your mind. Don't let them escape. We all know the feeling that we've just had a bright idea but we can't remember what it was. Jot down your first thoughts. You might decide to use a spider diagram technique to see if it helps you to think widely, to brainstorm the topic, in fact. You may remember that we introduced spider diagrams in Chapter 2 (see page 31) as a form of note-taking; they are also useful in helping you to generate ideas and then organize them before you start to write. Whether you use this technique or not, you absolutely must structure your ideas: the worst thing you can do at this stage (or any other) is to start to write and work through your notes until you've written them all up. You won't have produced notes in a logical sequence, because that isn't how we find information, and you can't easily see a pattern to your material just by sitting and looking at it.

> *Key point: select and organize your material before starting to write.*

An example of essay structure would be useful, and so we've taken a subject and shown how you might generate ideas about it, and then how you might structure it into a sensible, logical order. It's important to note that we've simplified and shortened the material for the purposes of this chapter.

Let's assume that a second-year student called Jenny Marshall is studying French, and has been given the following essay subject on which she's expected to write about 2000 words (in English, on this occasion!): *'Obsession is the main theme of Molière's plays. Discuss.'* We'll assume that Jenny has read several (not all!) of the plays of the seventeenth-century French playwright and some criticism as recommended in her booklist. She's also been to a couple of lectures on the plays. She therefore has a reasonable amount of knowledge, but it isn't focused; she needs to think what ideas she might use in her essay – not, at this stage, to structure them. She takes a sheet of plain paper, turns it into landscape position and writes in the middle 'obsession in Molière'. She then brainstorms the topic, deciding, for instance, that she must define 'obsession'; she must look at three or four plays at least and see what examples of obsession she can find and if they are of different types; she must look at other themes to see how important they might be, because of the word 'main' in the title; she must try to find out what Molière's purpose was in writing his plays, to see what link there might be to his themes. Jenny is aware that the endings of the plays tend to be rather weak and contrived: what happens to the obsessions then? Jenny notes these ideas on her spider diagram and, as often happens, they generate other questions, such as whether the social background of the time encouraged this kind of subject. She also realizes that she's been looking at the subject as though Molière had written novels: these are plays, and so their impact in the theatre will be important. Figure 3.1 shows what the spider diagram looks like so far.

Any of the ideas that Jenny has recorded at this point might be struck out as irrelevant, developed further or just touched on without development. These are her first thoughts only.

When Jenny feels reasonably sure that no more ideas are forthcoming at this stage, she takes another sheet of paper, puts the same words in a circle in the middle, marks the sheet 'Molière essay 2' so that it won't get mixed up with the previous effort and starts again. This time, she identifies what she's likely to include in the introduction (the definition, the plays she has selected and the structure of the essay) and she puts these ideas in related circles. She may decide not to write the introduction until the end of her essay, as it's often easier to identify the appropriate details when you've prepared the rest of the information; there's no rule that says you have to start at the beginning and, thanks to computers, nobody else will know the order in which the material was written.

Jenny then identifies the forms of obsession in the plays she's chosen and notices that, although in most cases the main character is the person with the obsession, in the case of *Tartuffe*, he is the hypocrite who plays on someone else's obsession. She makes a note of this without at present knowing if it will be useful. Hypocrisy is another theme, and she notes examples of this. The effect on the audience is linked to the endings, the humour and the playwright's intentions, which she must try to identify. Jenny is puzzled by one play, *Dom Juan*, as it doesn't seem to follow the usual pattern – its main character is more aware than others of what he is doing, even though he has obsessive sides to his character. She therefore gives it a circle of its own. A conclusion circle is also needed, showing that she will assess the subject and decide how far the statement is correct, looking at the reactions of a modern audience and her own. Figure 3.2 shows what the second spider diagram looks like.

It's now time to organize all these ideas into sections of the essay, at this stage giving them headings which identify them. It's worth looking at this aspect of the work for a moment or two. The essay itself probably won't have headings, but you need to use your spider diagram to help you to identify the sections, and it's easiest to do this by using short headings for yourself. At first, you may find that you have too

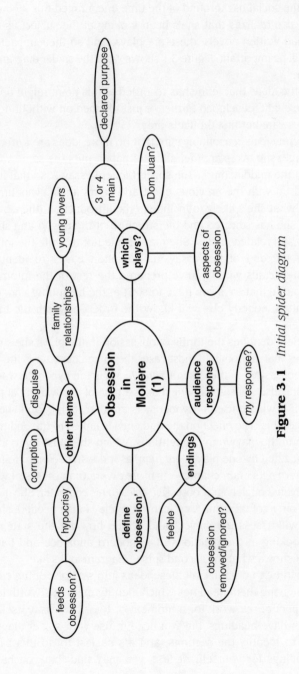

Figure 3.1 *Initial spider diagram*

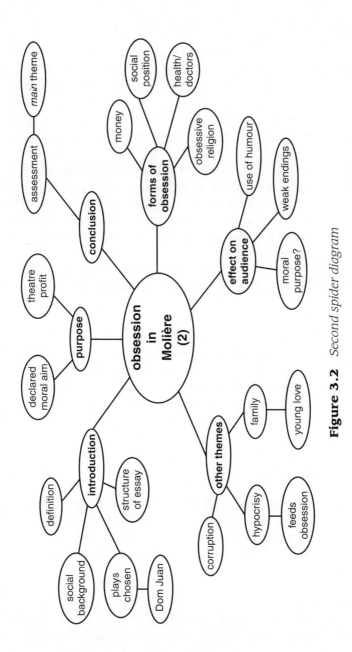

Figure 3.2 *Second spider diagram*

many, or too few, headings, and it doesn't matter: try out different ways of organizing them. You are simply finding a structure that works for your essay.

You may be one of the people who simply don't take to the spider diagram idea at all. Some people don't. It doesn't matter, except that you still need to have a good structure. Try to work from the title of the essay, planning headings as you think of different aspects of what you want to include. Play around with the headings, perhaps joining them together or dividing them, or changing the order, until you suddenly think, 'Yes, that works. That's how I'll organize my essay.' You may write down the headings or work on them in your mind, although you want to avoid the risk of forgetting an important idea, so it's probably better to make a note of them. When you're happy with the general structure, you can, within each section, decide on paragraphs. These are in some ways the basic building blocks of an essay and we'll say more about them in a little while (see pages 46–7).

However you've planned your essay, you will probably at this stage have a series of headings with a few brief reminders under each. Here are Jenny's:

- *Introduction*: include definition, the plays I'm going to discuss
- *Background and purpose*: Molière's stated moral purpose, demands of acting, professionalism, problems of censorship at the time
- *Forms of obsession*: think through plays and themes – religion, money, medicine and so on. *Dom Juan* different. What about endings?
- *Other themes*: family relationships, especially young love, disguise (this will bring the plays together)
- *Conclusion*: original audience reaction, modern audience. Yes, I agree about obsession.

From these headings, it's possible for Jenny to write her essay; in some ways, more than half the work has already been done and she can concentrate on the writing. It would take up far too much space to present the whole of Jenny's essay, but we can show how it might develop, section by section.

Introduction
This will include Jenny's definition of 'obsession', and the structure of her essay, stating which plays she will refer to. It will be one, or possibly two, paragraphs long.

Background and purpose

Jenny will move on to consider what types of play were popular at the time, the effects, if any, of censorship and the reactions of the authorities and Molière's declared purpose in writing his plays. His often stated moral purpose is worth stressing, as it has obvious links with the obsession theme, although he pronounces against the censorship of morals; however, Jenny remembers to add that as he was a professional actor as well as a playwright, motives such as publicity and money-making might be important, even if not stated! This section will be quite short, either one or two paragraphs, and will include some references to Jenny's background reading.

Forms of obsession

Jenny has moved to the main part of her essay, in which she will consider examples of obsession in the plays she has chosen and how they are shown through the characters; mainly there is one obsessional, with people of better sense trying to put a different set of values. She needs to avoid storytelling, or simply going from one play to the next without analysis, so she will need to decide whether there are different types of obsession or whether there is any chronological development in their portrayal. She adds a comment about the endings of the plays, showing briefly how the obsession illustrated is glossed over or disregarded in the final outcome. This is likely to be the longest section of the essay, perhaps half a dozen paragraphs altogether.

Other themes

The essay becomes more complex, as Jenny has to decide what the other themes are, and whether they are themselves of major importance or used simply to reveal the obsession. She must be able to move easily and confidently from play to play, again avoiding any temptation mechanically to discuss each in turn, but instead looking at them as a whole to find links between them. She may need two or three paragraphs for this section.

Dom Juan

Jenny still feels that *Dom Juan* doesn't quite fit the pattern, so she decides to give it a short paragraph of its own. As she comes to the conclusion that it doesn't undermine the main thesis of the essay, she doesn't want to spend long on it – but neither does she want to look as if she's hiding a counter-argument (she is absolutely right on both counts).

Conclusion

Jenny decides to go back to her earlier comment about Molière's purpose and discuss how members of the original audience might have reacted to his theme. She thinks about her own (necessarily limited) experience of the plays in the theatre, and feels that although the first audience, and she, would laugh, the obsession might remain as a talking point afterwards. In the light of the evidence she has presented, she agrees with the initial proposition. The conclusion will be one, or possibly two, paragraphs in length. The essay will probably have a short bibliography at the end.

We've spent a good deal of time on this essay, showing how the theme has been developed and the material selected and organized, because it's so important to plan and structure before you write. The same stages will apply however long or short your essay is and, to a large extent, the same pattern will be followed in your dissertation. If you get used to preparing to write in this way, you will gain credit for logical thinking, and you will have useful practice for your exams.

Paragraphs

We said earlier that paragraphs are, in a sense, the building blocks of an essay and it's worth looking at them a bit more closely. In Chapter 2, we defined a paragraph in general grammatical terms, but we'd now like to consider it as a unit in the essay. First of all, there's something we need to make clear: we've divided Jenny's essay into sections with headings. There is no reason why you shouldn't use headings in this way in an essay, but some lecturers don't like the style (check how yours feel before you write), and indeed you yourself may not like it, so don't feel either that you have to or that you mustn't. The important point is that these are sections of the essay and not paragraphs. If the 'Forms of obsession' section, for instance, were to be written as one paragraph, it would be more than a page long and very difficult to read; it would also move from one theme to another.

A paragraph signals to the reader that all the material in this block of text deals with one aspect of the subject. When the paragraph ends and a new one begins, readers understand that there is a change of aspect; this is a point when they can pause to take stock and prepare to start again with the new point of view or an opposing argument. So, while Jenny's study of the 'Other themes' in Molière's plays wouldn't necessarily have a new paragraph for each play, she would start a new paragraph when, for instance, she moved from considering hypocrisy to looking at the playwright's use of pretence and disguise – sometimes, but not always, linked to the major theme.

The length of your paragraphs will have an impact on the readability of your text. If your paragraphs are very long, say, most of a page, they will be difficult to read, not least because the reader will tend to look for a point at which to take stock. Sometimes you won't be able to avoid a paragraph of this sort, but don't make a habit of it. If you do, it may be because you haven't structured your ideas very sensibly. At the same time, avoid paragraphs which are only one sentence long; they are jerky and break up your ideas. Again, you can't always manage without them, but they should be very rare.

The effect of paragraphs should be cumulative: they reveal your ideas, develop your argument and show your conclusions. It's important, then, that your introductory paragraph(s) should start this process. You might define terms (as in the case of 'obsession'), clarify or if necessary modify the question (for example show which plays, poems or texts you are going to discuss) and let the reader know in what sequence you are going to deal with your topic. This last is particularly important: readers aren't mind-readers and they won't know how your argument is going to develop if you don't tell them; if you don't paragraph well, they may continue not to know even as they go through the essay.

The sequence of your paragraphs builds up your argument, taking it from stage to stage until you reach your conclusion. Don't be tempted to show your hand right at the beginning: Jenny mustn't start her essay by writing 'Obsession is clearly the major theme of Molière's plays' – before she's even presented any evidence. This is especially the case when personal feeling gets in the way: essay beginnings of the 'Anyone who thinks Shakespeare didn't write his plays must be mad' type must, on all occasions, be avoided. Show the conflicting points of view, allow the reader to see the relative strengths and weaknesses of your argument, save a good strong point in your favour until near the end, and then, as you draw your conclusion, readers will feel that they've been given a fair picture but you're probably right. Having said all this, we must add that there is sometimes a case for having a strong opening statement which you then develop, argue and in the end justify; however, in the case of a controversial topic like that in the example we've given, it's important to look at both sides of the question in a balanced way. You may occasionally be asked to justify a statement, in which case the strong opening could be effective.

> Key point: the sequence of your paragraphs shows the development of your argument and your conclusions.

Presentation

Your department will probably give you some guidance on the presentation of your essays, so check first to see if there are official guidelines; if not, the following comments might be useful.

A handwritten essay may be acceptable, although generally nowadays students have the opportunity to use a computer and of course this is preferable, not least from your point of view as it allows you to correct or move material freely. If you handwrite, use wide-lined paper and write on every other line, so that there is plenty of space for the marker's comments and corrections, and leave a good left-hand margin. Margins are especially important in a word-processed essay, as computer print is more densely packed than handwriting, and the marker will therefore have less space for comments if the margins are small.

If you are using a computer, use either 1.5 or double spacing, except for quotations which you inset as a separate block (see pages 29–30 for details of referencing). You can either indent new paragraphs or block them and leave an extra line between paragraphs. Titles of works which you mention in your essay should be in italics (underlined in hand-writing), and of course there is likely to be a bibliography at the end, set out consistently according to one of the recognized systems (see pages 29–30). Print your essay out in 12 point – anything smaller is harder to read and anything larger looks rather childish.

You will need to check your essay and we've given some guidance about checking in the section of this chapter which deals with dissertations (see pages 66–8). Make sure that the whole product looks tidy and well-organized, so that the first impression the marker gets is a good one. Don't staple the pages together, as the staple will certainly go through at least one important word on each page, but number the pages and see that the whole thing won't fall apart – a simple plastic folder is usually sufficient.

A final word: keep a copy of your essay. This may well be a require-ment in your continuous assessment but, in any case, it makes good sense. Work can be lost, by you or your tutor, or you may find you need to refer to it when it isn't in your possession. Photocopy it or back it up on the computer, and at least there's one thing you won't have to worry about.

> *Key point: check your essay and make a copy before you hand it in.*

Long essays

Some departments allow you to write a long essay as one unit in a particular course. You will need to check the details in your departmental handbook, but such essays tend to be about 7,000 or 8,000 words in length, with a bibliography which is unlikely to be included in the word count.

If you have the choice of writing a long essay or not, decide whether you think it's a good option for you. You may feel, for instance, that just because you've had experience of writing shorter essays, you would rather keep to what you know. On the other hand, for the same reason, you may be tempted to try something different. There is no particular merit in choosing either of these possibilities; it's much more important that you are comfortable with your choice.

A long essay requires more self-discipline than an ordinary essay. The topic should come out of your own interests, but it must be agreed with a member of staff, probably your tutor. You will get help in choosing an appropriate supervisor, and you will then have a set number of meetings at which you can show the work so far and get help and advice. Nevertheless, you will work largely on your own, and with the space you have, you will need to develop and sustain a substantial argument based on your own reading and research. You will also have to organize your time wisely, so that you can read enough, plan properly, write and check in an orderly manner.

The needs of the long essay make it an appropriate choice for people who want to write a dissertation (if it's optional), or who are interested in more advanced research in the future. If you are the kind of student who wants to get by with the minimum of work, the long essay is probably not a good choice – but of course you aren't like that, or you wouldn't be using this book.

> *Key point: decide whether a long essay, if it's an option, is right for you.*

A great deal of the advice we've given for writing a long essay is the same as that for a dissertation, so if you're writing a long essay, please also read the section about dissertation writing (pages 55–68).

▶ Reports

You may not have met report writing in the past, and you may not need it during your course; if this is so, you may skip this section or just skim it to get a general idea of what a report is. You may come back to it when you are at work, as reports are a common form of writing in many areas of employment. You may, however, find that you are asked to write a report if your course includes a 'business' element, for instance if you are reading a subject including or combined with management, or if you take a unit which looks at business communication.

So, how is a report different from an essay? Both are structured, but a report has a visible structure, being divided into numbered sections and subsections, each with its own heading. There is a basic format to all reports: the subject is introduced, the evidence is presented, and then there is some kind of comment, usually conclusions drawn on the basis of the evidence, or recommendations made as a result of the evidence. There's also a basic rule, that the evidence is given as impartially as possible (this has implications for the style of writing) but the comments are your own and therefore subjective.

Reports are often written in response to a request for information, or in order to persuade the reader to a particular decision or action; they may also be a record of actions taken, especially if somebody else has to continue the work. You can see how important they are in a business or management setting, and how useful it is if you have the opportunity to write at least one report as part of your course.

Let's assume that Steve Hopkinson, an undergraduate studying classics, has a vacation job for two months as a sales assistant in the local bookshop. He's enjoyed the work and on the whole has done it well, and so his employer asks him if, before he finishes, he would write a short report summing up his experiences and making any useful suggestions for future temporary staff. So, about a week before he leaves the shop, Steve starts to gather ideas together for his report. He uses the spider diagram technique with which you are now familiar in order to record and then to sort out his thoughts.

First, there will be an introduction, in which he will explain that he is a final-year classics student, working in August and September as a sales assistant in the bookshop, which, of course, he will identify. He will also explain what the manager has asked him to do.

Steve thinks back to his first days at work, and notes the training he was given: a general introduction to the layout of the shop and the various aspects of the job; use of the till; work on the computer which records both books in print and the current stock; and a bit of customer care. This was all useful and sensibly given, and his colleagues have been friendly and helpful when he hasn't known what to do in a particular situation. This note reminds him, however, of one difficulty: on a Thursday evening, when the shop was open for late-night shopping, he had a very difficult and offensive customer, and it hadn't been easy to get help. This gives him two ideas for a Recommendations section: perhaps the shop needs more staff on duty on Thursday evenings, and perhaps he might have had more introduction to customer care (a topic he'd always seen as obvious, as he's a friendly, outgoing young man, but which he now knows has more complexity than he'd ever realized). He will also record his hours and conditions of work, which seem reasonable, and he will make a note of one of the benefits of this employment, that the manager has been willing to give him different responsibilities so that he can learn as much as possible while he's on the job. As Steve is interested in publishing as a career, he feels that the knowledge he has gained of the book trade will be useful to him in the long term.

The spider diagram seems more or less complete, but Steve recognizes that he should add his own assessment of the experience. He's learnt practical skills (the till, the computer), personal skills (customer relations, working with colleagues) and, he thinks, some self-discipline (getting to work for 8.45 every morning, especially every other Saturday, did not come easily to him). He would recommend the job to another student. Nevertheless, he feels he should include both the suggestions he's thought of. The spider diagram now looks like Figure 3.3.

How can this material now be turned into a report? Steve can identify his main headings from his diagram, as:

1 Introduction
2 Hours and conditions of work
3 Training
4 Work duties and responsibilities
5 Work experience gained
6 Conclusions
7 Recommendations

University of Ulster LIBRARY

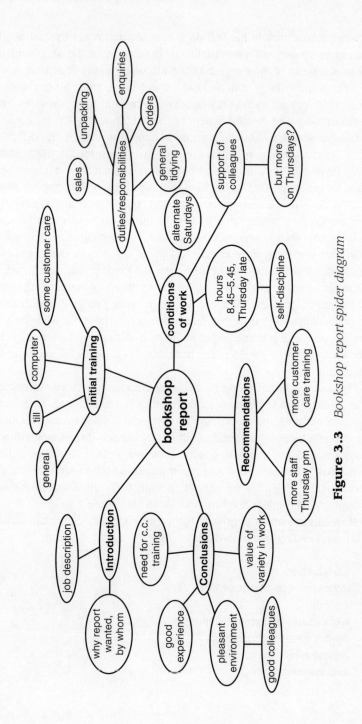

Figure 3.3 *Bookshop report spider diagram*

On second thoughts, Steve decides that his second main heading, Hours and conditions of work, is really part of the Introduction. He therefore makes it a subsection, so that he has:

1 Introduction
1.1 Personal background
1.2 Hours and conditions of work

and he adjusts the other headings accordingly. Under the second heading, he uses four subheadings:

2 Training
2.1 General work introduction
2.2 Computer training
2.3 Till training
2.4 Customer care

Under his Conclusions heading, Steve will assess the evidence he has presented, most of which is favourable, but with the reservation he has about customer care. He will then make his Recommendations, including the suggestion of extra training and more staffing on Thursday evenings, and also the general recommendation that, as he thinks the experience has been most useful, another undergraduate might be employed in the same way in the following year.

Layout of reports
You will notice that each of Steve's main headings is shown in bold type; this will hold true throughout the report, so that section **7 Recommendations** will match the earlier headings. He has used the decimal form of numbering, so that each main number can be divided into as many subordinate numbers as are needed (in spite of the name 'decimal', he isn't limited to ten). If he wanted to subdivide again, then the system would repeat itself, for example:

1.2 Hours and conditions of work
    1.2.1 Weekdays excluding Thursdays
    1.2.2 Thursdays
    1.2.3 Saturdays

As 1.2 isn't a main heading, it isn't bold; the sub-subdivisions, 1.2.1 and so on, are indented to show that they are a new level of heading. The only rule is that each form of heading should be clear and consistent; you might choose a different form, such as bold upper case followed by bold lower case, especially if you have a good deal of material to organize. You might, in this case, need to go as far as 1.1.1.1, but don't have more than four numbers at any stage; you're unlikely to need more than two in a short report.

Summaries

Many reports have a short summary at the beginning, so that the reader gets the full impact of the message of the report. Steve probably won't write one for his report, as it's unlikely to be more than two or three pages in length, but if your report were to be seven or eight pages or more, the reader would be helped by a short summary. Let's assume that Steve is so carried away by his report that he decides to add a summary. He will need to include, very briefly, why the report is needed, the essentials of what he wants to say and, most important of all, his conclusions and recommendations. As the whole report is short, his Summary is unlikely to be more than about 100 words. It might be something like this.

Summary

Steve Hopkinson, temporary sales assistant at James French & Co, booksellers, has been asked by the manager to provide a short report about his work experience. His training, hours and conditions of work have been satisfactory, but he would recommend more training in customer care, and an extra member of staff to work on Thursday evenings.

Steve has gained useful experience, in practical work and human relations, and a measure of self-discipline, through this employment. It is hoped that a similar opportunity will be extended to another student in the following year.

As you will see, this Summary gives readers an overview of the report, so that if they had no time to read the whole document, they would still get a good idea of what Steve had said. A summary often helps readers who will afterwards read the whole report to get a quick first impression which will help to focus the essentials in their minds. If in your report you are trying to persuade your readers of something, a decision or an action, the summary is particularly useful.

Style of reports

Reports are formal documents, and must be written in an appropriate style. On the whole, don't use 'I' or 'you' in a report, or abbreviations like 'don't', although an exception might be used for Steve's very personal report to his manager: he might choose to write 'I', but his style should generally be formal and impersonal. Even when you are giving your own assessment of the situation, keep your style as impersonal as you can (you will notice that Steve doesn't refer to himself directly in the Summary given above). Obviously, you wouldn't use slang or unnecessary jargon in a report, but don't be tempted to write in a pompous way, either; the effort to be impersonal sometimes makes people resort to legal-type expressions such as 'hereinafter' or 'prior to' (meaning 'before'). It's painful to read such writing, which does nothing to improve your mark.

> *Key point: reports have numbered headings and often a short Summary at the beginning; the writing style is formal.*

Preparing a report

If you find that you have to write a report as part of your course or, like Steve, for some other reason, remember that you need to organize your ideas first, and preferably decide on the headings you will use, before you begin to write. All the best reports are prepared in this way; you want to avoid getting halfway through the writing and then thinking of a better way to structure your information. Get a good structure first and then you can concentrate on the writing – much as you would with an essay, in fact.

▶ Dissertations

The longest, and in a way the most important, piece of extended writing you are likely to have to do during your course is almost certainly your dissertation. In this section, we'll give you some help with this task, but you must remember that faculties and departments vary in their requirements and of course different subjects need different approaches. Please look at the information you've been given, or ask what is available to help you, and always give your own local instructions priority over what we say. In so far as you have choices to make, or to reinforce what you've been told, read on.

There is one other proviso: we're writing primarily for undergraduates and our advice is geared to their dissertations. What we say is also of general application to postgraduate dissertations, but we're not concerned with PhD theses, which are based on original research and therefore need a rather different approach.

So, you're going to write a dissertation for the first time, and you're wondering how to begin. Look at the parameters of your choice of topic. Your departmental brochure will probably tell you that your choice must fall within a reasonable definition of the subject; for instance, if you are studying German, your dissertation must fall into one of the areas in which your department has expertise, such as German language and literature, and the history, culture, politics and institutions of German-speaking countries. Within these categories, you are likely to choose either a library-based topic, concentrating on literature or history, or an information-gathering topic, which would involve you in visits, interviews, use of the media and so on.

We've used German as an example, but the same principles apply to most subjects in arts and humanities. Your topic must be within the teaching range of your department, not least so that you can have an appropriate supervisor. You will then need to consider what type of work appeals to you most: do you especially enjoy library work, or would you prefer the opportunity to talk to people and use modern sources of information such as newspapers or television? (Obviously, you may not have such a choice, but most subjects lend themselves to a similar division; in history, for example, you might choose to examine specific primary source material, or you might prefer to consider critically a particular historical issue or problem.)

You will now have the most difficult decision: what are you going to choose for the subject of your dissertation? Start by reflecting on the various courses you've taken over the past year or two. What have you most enjoyed? What has really captured your interest? What did you get your best marks for? This is a good place to start, as you are going to spend a great deal of time on your dissertation, and you need to choose a topic which will hold your interest, so that as far as possible, you enjoy working on it. If you become bored, you will lose motivation and so the incentive to produce a good dissertation.

It isn't a choice for you alone. One or more of your lecturers will probably be in charge of organizing dissertations and will give you general advice; when you have some idea of the area in which you would like to work, you will be given a supervisor with expertise in your chosen field, and he or she will guide you through the whole process of preparing your dissertation, being ready to help if you run into difficulties. In some departments, you can approach a possible supervisor for yourself; remember that supervising a dissertation involves time and effort, and it will help if your supervisor is someone whose lectures you've enjoyed and with whom you have a certain amount of rapport. You may find that the response you meet is less than enthusiastic if you've regularly skipped lectures and handed work in late.

Narrowing down the subject

You've now got in mind a topic for your dissertation, and you've had some encouragement to make you feel optimistic that it's a sensible one to choose. Almost inevitably, at this early stage, you will have made the mistake of trying to cover too large a subject. It's an easy error: you feel that if you choose a very small, specific area, you might not find enough information. Almost everyone feels like this, but it's highly unlikely to be the case. Generally speaking, the smaller and more precise your choice of subject, the easier it will be to produce something really interesting, perhaps even original. You may not be able to make such a decision straightaway: you may need to start with a wider topic and narrow it down as you talk to people about it and start to look at the literature available.

> Key point: ask for advice about your dissertation topic, narrow it down and clarify your objectives.

The library or libraries at your disposal now play an important part in your preparation. You aren't asked at this stage to add to the sum of human knowledge; that will come later if you decide to write a PhD thesis – which, as we said earlier, is beyond the scope of this book. You do, however, need to find out what other people have said about your possible topic and, if you can, see a theme or a synthesis of ideas which hasn't been handled in quite this way before. The more you read, the more likely it is that you'll be able to narrow your subject down to the point at which you can handle the material available and write it up within the word limit you've been given.

You must, of course, check the word limit. In most departments, an undergraduate dissertation is about 10,000 to 15,000 words in length, and a postgraduate dissertation about 20,000 to 30,000 words. This will seem like a vast number of words, but most students find that their main problem is not that they have too little material to reach the limit, but that they have to fit all they want to say into this restriction. Nobody will count the words in your writing, but examiners have an instinct born of long experience in these matters, and it isn't wise to be far off the mark, as you may be heavily penalized for using too many words.

You will probably have to provide your supervisor with draft material: a provisional title, an indication of your objectives, a note of some of the main sources of your reading and a synopsis of what you want to say and how you want to say it. Any of this may change and it's wise to discuss your ideas at an early stage; your supervisor will almost certainly make helpful comments about your ideas, but he or she has to have some basic material to work on. Read critically and make sure that you make a note of everything you read: you will need to be able to look at it again at a later stage of your work and probably include the details in your bibliography.

Identifying objectives

You are trying to establish sensible objectives for your dissertation, and just deciding on a narrow topic which interests you, useful though it is, isn't enough. You can't afford to be simply descriptive; you have to show your skills of selection and analysis. To do this, you need to have a focus, often in the form of questions to which you are going to find answers.

This can be a good way of identifying your objectives: why does something happen, under what circumstances does it happen, are there exceptions, what were the influences at work at the time? The answers to these questions will become clear (if they don't, that in itself might be an interesting topic) as you study the subject further, but asking the questions helps to focus your thinking and so give you the basis for a dissertation structure. If we think back for a moment to Jenny's Molière essay, discussed earlier in this chapter (pages 40–6), you can see how this would work even in a short piece of writing: when does Molière show obsession and why, are there exceptions, are there other themes, are they equally important? These would be some of the key questions that Jenny set out to answer.

You are carrying out the same kind of exercise in beginning to plan your dissertation. It's often easier to think of questions to ask than of possible material to include and, at this stage, you need as much help as possible in narrowing down your subject and deciding how to focus your approach.

When you feel that you are beginning to clarify your objectives, write them down. This is not just because you can then discuss them with your supervisor, but because the very act of writing will help to crystallize your ideas. You may amend your objectives later, but you'll have a basis for your work.

We've mentioned your supervisor again. As you narrow your topic, it may change its focus and your supervisor needs to know your current thinking. Find out exactly what help is available from your tutor or supervisor, and, at this early stage especially, make sure that you don't make radical changes without getting agreement. You may work together to decide on the exact wording of the title, and you may be given further bibliographical help once this is established. If you are taking a combined degree course and your topic involves both subjects, you will almost certainly have a supervisor in each department; again, find out how this will work in your case and keep both supervisors informed of your decisions.

Dissertation timetable

One aspect of the help you may need is advice about setting yourself a dissertation timetable. You will be given a final date by which your work has to be submitted and to a certain extent you can work backwards from that, choosing a sensible date for completing the word processing, then the checking and, if possible, allowing time for a friend or relative to read the dissertation through for small errors you might have missed (for a more detailed discussion of checking, see pages 66–8). You may have deadlines along the way: some will be official, such as the date by which you have to hand in your synopsis, and some will be specific to you, such as the date by which you hope to have all the interviews completed, or by which you want to start the actual writing.

Try to make your timetable realistic – if it's hopelessly idealistic, you won't keep it. If it's a sensible programme but you still find one of your dates won't work, then readjust it – at least you've recognized the problem. Always allow yourself extra spaces, gaps in which you can catch up on other work, revise for exams, or just take a break from the stress of academic work.

> *Key point: set yourself a realistic dissertation timetable, with extra spaces for emergencies.*

In most three-year courses, you will be given a strong recommendation that you do as much work on your dissertation as possible during the Easter vacation, summer term and summer vacation of your second year. The workload in the final year is likely to be a heavy one, and you can't afford to have to spend too much time catching up on dissertation work. If you are spending a year abroad as part of your course, then you have a good opportunity during that year to gather your information, organize it and get on with the writing. Two words of advice: keep in touch with your supervisor via email during the year, as you mustn't move too far without checking that you are approaching the topic in the right way, and always keep a copy of material you send back to your supervisor. No post is perfect and international post can be subject to delays or disruption. Come to think of it, that's good advice for internal post, too.

Dissertation structure
It's difficult for us to give you an outline structure for your dissertation, as it will depend on your subject and chosen topic, but we've given you advice about organizing material, and a dissertation is much the same as other forms of writing, except longer.

You will probably find that the general format will be something like the one we've suggested below, but we can't stress too strongly that you must check the requirements of your own department.

- **Title page**, including your name and the date of submission
- **Preface**, in which you may wish to describe the context in which you carried out your work, or to make any acknowledgements for help and advice received
- **Table of contents**, showing all the chapter or section titles with page references. You may need to list tables, maps and so on under a separate heading
- **List of abbreviations used**, including books commonly referred to, for example in a history dissertation, you would include *VCH* for *Victoria County History*
- **Introduction** to the dissertation topic
- **Main text** of the dissertation, divided into chapters or sections, each with an appropriate title

- **Conclusion**, assessing your material and perhaps discussing further work
- **Appendices**, including material which is supplementary to the main text, or which would not fit easily into a chapter; each appendix should have a title
- **Bibliography**, which may be one sequence of references, or sub-divided (for example in history, it would probably be divided into primary sources, subdivided if appropriate into manuscript sources and printed sources, and secondary sources). Check the exact format used in your department.

Within this kind of framework, you will have your chapter headings showing how your material is organized. We said earlier in talking about essays (see pages 39–40) that it's essential to plan before starting to write, and of course you will organize all your ideas, first into an overall pattern and then chapter by chapter; this may take time, but it will do wonders for your confidence to have a structure you're happy with, and your supervisor is happy with, before you start to write.

There's one other useful planning exercise we'd like to recommend, and that has to do with allocating words.

Word allocation

As soon as you are reasonably sure of the outline plan of your dissertation and have your own headings, look again at the total number of words you are allowed and, very approximately, allocate an appropriate number to each chapter or major section, all the way through your outline. Deal in hundreds of words – you can't hope to be exact. If you can, ask your supervisor to comment on your word allocation – it's always useful to have a second opinion. (An average A4 page of type, double spaced and 12 point, has about 350 words in it.)

This is a very important step. As you write up your dissertation, you will be keeping the word allocation in mind. Of course, it will often turn out to be wrong – you couldn't know for sure at the beginning how much information you would have at each stage of the writing. But it allows you to ask questions, and that is its great benefit.

If you used far more words than you expected in a particular chapter, ask yourself:

- Have I included irrelevant material?
- Have I gone into too much detail at times?

- Am I repeating material unnecessarily?
- Is my style wordy and rambling?

If you honestly answer 'no' to each of these questions, then ask:

- Am I totally justified in using so many words in this chapter, was my original estimate wrong, and where do I save words in order to accommodate all these extra words?

If you used far fewer words than you expected, ask yourself:

- Have I left out something important?
- Have I treated some aspect of the work superficially?
- Have I justified all that I've said, with closely reasoned argument and supporting evidence?
- Are all my sentences grammatical, or am I tending to write in note form?

If you honestly answer 'no' to each of these questions, then ask:

- Am I totally justified in using so few words in this chapter, was my original estimate wrong, and where can I use the extra words at my disposal most effectively?

The great advantage of going through this process is that at each stage you are asking questions. The worst thing you can do (and we write from experience of seeing this happen) is to write up 9,000 words of a 10,000 word dissertation, and then realize that you have 5,000 words left to write. The only way out of this predicament is to start again with a better structure, but who would ever have time for that? If you use the questions above, you will know at each stage how many words you've used and how many you have left, and you will also know how the information is to be fitted into the number of words.

> *Key point: allocate the number of words available and check how many you have used at each stage.*

When you start writing, you will probably feel very nervous. It can feel very final (although of course it isn't) to commit words to the keyboard.

Don't feel that you have to start at the beginning. Choose a comparatively easy section, however short, and write that first. There is a great psychological hurdle to be overcome in starting, and you will feel very much more positive and optimistic once you have written something. You may also want to draft-write at least some parts of your dissertation and discuss them with your supervisor. Check at what points it's acceptable for you to do this. Back up your work at regular intervals and especially before you leave it overnight; keep a copy of any work you print out and hand in to your supervisor; it's much easier for you to correct and copy your work than it was in the past, and so use the computer facilities available to you.

Writing style

A dissertation is a formal document, and your writing style should reflect this. It's all too easy, especially as you seem to have such a large word allocation, to ramble or include irrelevant detail about your own reactions to the work you've done. Be careful to avoid such traps, as they will tend to trivialize your writing.

Inevitably, you will use a number of conventions that apply in your subject. Find out what is appropriate, by asking or looking at the major journals published in your field of study. In general, though, use abbreviations which are widely recognized in your subject and don't make up your own. Whole numbers under and including ten are written as words, unless they are associated with units, such as sums of money, when figures are used. Round numbers are always written as words ('There were about a thousand people at the scene'). Inclusive numbers should show the fewest possible figures, for example 134–9, 1967–8, although in writing 'teen' figures, it's usual to repeat the 1, as in 1914–18.

Don't put a hyphen in twentieth century (or similar), unless you're using it as an adjective ('twentieth-century women').

Unless you are told otherwise, write dates in a clear and modern style, as 17 February 2003, with no punctuation. Don't abbreviate the names of days or months, and write the year in full, as 2003 rather than 03. More general abbreviations tend to have their own rules, although the modern tendency is to avoid full stops (VCH, UN and so on).

These are just some modern conventions which you can follow if you are given no conflicting guidance. Your writing style can be summed up in 12 guidelines, which we'll set out for you. It goes without saying that your grammar, spelling and punctuation must be correct.

Checklist for dissertation style

1 Keep your sentence length under control
2 Keep your paragraph length under control
3 Use logical connections such as 'therefore', 'moreover' correctly
4 Follow the conventions of your subject in layout, names and abbreviations
5 Don't become personal, emotional or chatty
6 Don't address the reader directly as 'you'
7 Avoid referring directly to yourself as 'I'
8 Don't use abbreviations such as 'don't' or 'can't'
9 Use precise language whenever possible, not 'fairly often', 'quite a lot', and so on
10 Write concisely and avoid waffle
11 If you use illustrations, identify them with a title and give your source
12 Check all you write, including corrections

You will, of course, also need to read Chapter 4 of this book, for much more detailed help with good writing style.

Key point: write in a formal style, following the conventions of your subject.

Abstracts

You may be asked to prepare an abstract of about 300 to 500 words to be put at the front of your dissertation. As you write the rest of your material, remember that if you have to do this, you will need to make a separate note of any aspects that seem to you of particular importance in each chapter. You may have to summarize the content of your dissertation a chapter at a time, or you may need to give an overall summary, stressing what is of particular significance in your work. It's a good idea to look at two or three past dissertations in your department to see how previous students presented their abstracts.

Always draft your abstract with more words than you are allowed, say 500–700. Next, check what can be cut out, and also whether you have used unnecessary words or repetition, or included too much detail. You should be able to work on your draft until you get it to the right length – don't go over the number of words given, but if you're slightly below the number, it's unlikely to matter.

Your abstract will almost certainly be the first part of your dissertation to be read by your examiner. It's worth taking time with it, and making sure that the first impression is a good one.

Plagiarism

We've already given you advice about recording the source of your notes, and about writing references (see pages 28 and 29), but we're going to come back to the subject of plagiarism here because it's so important and writing your dissertation is probably the occasion when it's most easy to get it wrong.

As we've said before, plagiarism is a form of theft and therefore the penalties are severe; if you are found to have used someone else's ideas or words without acknowledgement, you could lose the mark for the whole dissertation, or even be excluded from the university. It isn't worth the risk. In any case, you will almost certainly have to hand in with your dissertation a statement that the work is all your own.

We can give you some hints to help you avoid the risk of plagiarism, but if you aren't sure about any particular piece of information, always ask; this applies particularly to the awkward 'grey area' between material which is said to be 'in the public domain', that is, so well known that you don't need to give a reference, and information which is specific to one source and therefore has to be acknowledged.

As you write notes for your dissertation, either rephrase the material in your own words and make a note of where the idea came from, or copy the words exactly in some way that means you will always know that they weren't your own, such as in a different colour, in inverted commas or whatever system you choose. Be consistent, so that you recognize your own system every time, and always make a note of all the details of your source, including the page reference so that you can find it again quickly if you need to do so.

An essay or dissertation must be in your own words unless you are deliberately quoting, so if you do quote, the exact extent of the quotation must be obvious; if it's a few words, put them in inverted commas; if there is a whole line of print or more, set the quotation out as a separate paragraph and indent it.

If you use someone else's idea without quoting directly, introduce it in a way which makes this clear, such as 'Smith states that ...', or 'Robinson's argument is that ...'. Again, make sure that you have all the necessary details to give in your bibliography. Never 'adapt' someone else's words to pass them off as your own. This applies to illustrations and diagrams, too: it isn't enough to make a few small changes and hope that the reader will think that it's your original work.

If you use notes which belong to somebody else, for instance taken by a friend on the same course, check where the material comes from *yourself* – don't rely on another person's guess about the origin of the material. Never allow someone else to write some of your dissertation for you, and never download material straight from a website into your text. It would be easy to forget that the words weren't your own; you must know where all your material comes from, and you must give the source of website material just as you would any other.

All work that you have referred to or quoted from must be acknowledged in the text and must appear in your bibliography.

This sounds like a burden for the writer, but once you establish your own ground rules for references and quotations, you will use them automatically, and a potentially serious problem will have been avoided.

Key point: follow your departmental guidelines for references and quotations; you must know where all your information comes from and acknowledge it as appropriate.

▶ Revision and checking

Revision is less a stage than a continual process as you prepare your material. Every time you talk to your supervisor, you may have to revise some aspect of what you are preparing. Further reading or discussion may affect your conclusions; the work itself may lead you to revise some aspects of your writing. Be flexible enough to do this, even though it seems to be a great nuisance at the time. You don't want to realize when it's too late that there were ideas that you should have taken note of, but didn't.

Checking is much more of a last effort, but so important that you must leave time for it. Nowadays most students write their dissertations straight onto the computer; this saves time and allows you to move material round as you see fit, but it also presents a problem. We are all the very worst people to check our own writing. We know what we wanted to say, and so that's what we read, even if in fact we've written something else.

The first level of checking is to use the computer spellcheck (making sure that it uses English rather than American forms), and to read what's on the screen. This will draw your attention to some typing or spelling errors, but not, of course, to those which make a different word: these may be words which are similar in form but used differently, such as *principle/principal*; they may be words which sound the same, such as *weather/whether*; they may result in nasty grammatical errors, such as a *their/there* confusion. None of these will be found by your computer, and they are very difficult to see from a reading of the screen. The most notorious of these confusions is *not/now*, which reverses the meaning, as in 'This point of view is now discredited'/'This point of view is not discredited'.

The next level of checking is from a printout. This has advantages: it's a more normal way of reading than from a screen, and you can see a much wider area of your work, comparing several pages at once if you need to do so. If you can, leave your work alone for 48 hours and then read it again – you're much more likely to notice mistakes than if you read it straightaway.

Check each section of your writing in this way, and make a note of decisions you've made; these may in themselves be unimportant, such as whether you spell *organise* with an *s* or a *z*, but you need to be consistent. Check also that you are using abbreviations and capital letters in a consistent way, and again note your decisions, as otherwise you won't remember them.

You may want to ask a friend or colleague to read your dissertation. If you can, persuade someone with little knowledge of the subject to read it for the expression, especially if you aren't writing in your first language; then, perhaps on an exchange basis, try to get someone who does know at least something about the subject to read it to see if there are any obvious errors or omissions.

All this takes time, and you need to allow for the checking stage in your preliminary planning. When you've corrected all the errors that have been pointed out to you, we're sorry, but you need to check the whole thing again. It's surprising how often correcting one error creates another. When you've printed out or photocopied the correct number of copies of your dissertation, check that all the pages are there in the right order. Photocopiers can skip a page and printers can jam. You have (of course) numbered your pages, so it shouldn't take long to complete this stage of checking.

Key point: check your work thoroughly.

Time runs out, and checking is a very boring task. It's worth remembering that examiners are only human, and if they see obvious errors as they start to read your dissertation, they will assume that you are a careless, unprofessional person, and that therefore the content of your work will be slapdash too. If this seems unfair, think of it like this: your future employers will react in exactly the same way.

4 Good Writing Style

As you have read the articles and books recommended during your course, you will have noticed that the presentation and style of writing varies greatly. Some writers seem to discourage study by the very look of their pages, which are densely packed with information, in small print and with little margin space. You may also find that the writing itself seems unfriendly: one common effect of this is to make you reread sentences, not because they contain complex material, but because it's difficult to work out the meaning at once.

Other writing has the opposite effect: you expected to find the topic difficult, but as soon as you started to read, you were encouraged to continue, first by the use of space and an attractive font, and then by the flow of the words and sentences, so that you were surprised how much information you absorbed in a relatively short time.

Your readers – at present mainly the staff who teach you – have exactly the same reactions. They have to read a great deal of student writing, and they naturally want the experience to be as rapid and pleasurable as possible. Nevertheless, they are under a professional obligation to tackle what you have written and assess it. Later, when you are employed, the problem will be more stark: if your writing is going to take a long time and much dedication to read, nobody will bother. Your influence on your colleagues and senior managers will wane and promotion will pass you by. This might seem like exaggeration, but it isn't; the need to communicate clearly, accurately and effectively in writing has never been greater, and all your knowledge and skill will make little impact if you can't write well.

In this chapter, we shall look first at the need to be accurate, that is, to use the language in such a way that you make your meaning clear to your readers without ambiguity or uncertainty. This will involve using words and sentences in a precise way, and ensuring that the result is readable. There is a bonus for you in this: once you can use the language clearly and accurately, you will find that you achieve power over it, and that you can influence your readers just by the way in which you write. You will be writing effectively, and this is a rare and precious skill.

Having introduced the chapter as a guide to good writing, we must add that, of course, this isn't a basic grammar book; if you are unsure of the rules of punctuation and syntax, you will need a different book, perhaps one of those listed in the bibliography. We shall, however, discuss ways of improving your style, and give specific examples of common errors to guide you.

▶ Appropriate writing

Writing has to have a context. There are few absolute rules for every style and every readership; you have to choose what fits the task in hand. If you are writing for a close friend and the subject is an evening out, there are very few rules; indeed, your grammar may be slipshod and your punctuation almost non-existent, and it won't matter, as long as your friend gets the message. However, there is a limit shown in that 'as long as': if the writing is so casual that the meaning is obscured, then your reader has a right to be irritated.

In this section, we'll look at the same information written in a variety of styles, none of them 'right' or 'wrong', but each appropriate for particular readers and occasions, and we'll comment on the main features of each. We've chosen four ways of writing that cover most occasions, but of course none is totally self-contained, and you may want to move between them or use a compromise in order to get a particular response from your readers. It will be your judgement which will decide on the appropriate style for your particular purpose, but it's useful to have several styles at your command.

> Key point: choose your style according to your readers and the context in which you're writing.

We've chosen to use a short passage about choice of style, and to show how it might be written in four different ways: as instructions, in a formal academic style, in a less formal style and, more or less, as speech (it's not easy to show exactly how we speak, as so much depends on inflexions of voice).

1 Instructional style

> Consider the following when choosing an appropriate style:
>
> - readers and their expectations
> - the purpose of the writing
> - the context in which it will be read
> - the potential lifespan of the writing.

Comment
If you are asked to write instructions for someone to follow, you will need to keep your style brief and to the point. The instruction itself will be written in the imperative ('consider'), and the details which follow will be clearly identified and precise. It's worth noting that if your instructions have to be carried out in a particular order, you will number each stage, to emphasize that the order matters. Otherwise, as in the passage above, you can use bullet points. In either case, this is a very spare style of writing, as any elaboration might distract from the key message.

2 Formal academic style

> In choosing an appropriate style, the writer should consider the readers and their expectations. They may be children or young adults; they may be mature and highly educated; they might require entertainment or complex information. In each case, they need to relate to a particular way of writing, feeling neither intimidated nor patronized.
>
> The purpose of writing is also an important consideration. It might be purely ephemeral, conveying trivial information, or it might be a work of reference with an extended lifespan. In the latter case, it would be unwise to use expressions which are only the fashion of the moment, as they might become unintelligible as well as a potential embarrassment for the writer.

Comment
This is the traditional textbook way of writing, impersonal and formal. You will notice that there are no abbreviations such as it's or wouldn't, as such expressions are written out in full. The punctuation is formal (notice the use of semi-colons), as is the sentence structure, as you can see in the 'neither...nor' construction. The language chosen is also formal,

both in the number of long words, such as *expectations*, *ephemeral*, *potential*, and the way in which they are joined (*in the latter case…*). You may decide (or be told) that this is an appropriate style in which to write an essay or dissertation. It is certainly the traditional style of academic writing.

3 Informal writing

> Before you start to write, think about the style you're going to use. It must suit its readers, so that they feel comfortable in reading it: if it seems childish or impossibly difficult to understand, they will soon give up. Are they to be entertained or educated? If you're writing just to get an immediate response, you might choose a casual style, including slang or current jargon, but if you want to be read with pleasure fifty years from now, it's wise to be more formal and avoid any expression which has a short shelf life.

Comment
This is closer to the style we've adopted in this book. It's personal (you, we), and uses expressions which are in some ways closer to speech than formal writing ('soon give up' and, perhaps slightly tongue in cheek, 'a short shelf life'). There is a direct question, which would be unusual in more formal writing, and contractions such as 'you're'. You may want to write an essay in this style, but check first that it doesn't irritate the person who is going to mark it. Nowadays, people tend to write less formally than in the past, as we have done, but you have to keep the needs, and perhaps the personality, of the reader in mind. Don't choose this style unless you know it's acceptable.

4 Spoken style

> So you're going to start writing. *How* are you going to write? Well, let's have a look at style, for instance, the *way* in which you write. It's going to depend on a lot of things – who's going to read it, for instance, and *why* you're writing. There's a big difference between writing for children and writing, let's say, a student textbook. Or a learned article, or the sort of book you read on the train going home from work. *Who*'s going to read it, and *why* and *when* they're going to read it, all these will have an effect on how you write. It's no good using slang that everyone knows now, if you want to be read in fifty years' time.

Comment

This is, more or less, how we speak, and you will see that it's different from even the informal style of writing. We've shown emphasis by italicizing the words we'd stress just by our tone of voice; in writing, we have to emphasize by sentence structure and choice of words. The punctuation is simple (you can't *say* a semi-colon) and the sentences are short, indeed, they are not necessarily grammatical sentences at all. The audience is addressed directly as 'you', and involved in the communication ('let's have a look'), and the language is informal ('big', 'the sort of book you read'). This style tends to be wordy, partly because some repetition is needed for the listeners, and partly because we use 'flow words', extra words such as the 'so' at the beginning, which mean nothing but help the flow of words.

Later in the book (see pages 112–14), we'll be looking in more detail at the need to use spoken language in talking to an audience; the writing style we discuss in the rest of this chapter is appropriate for university writing in most contexts. You may be writing an essay, a dissertation or an article for publication: the way you write will have slight variations but it will essentially be similar. It will be clear and unambiguous; it will also usually be formal, closer to the second example above than any of the others. In order to achieve this, you will need to use the rules in a way which hardly matters if you are speaking or writing a note to a friend.

> *Key point: academic writing must be clear, unambiguous and generally in a formal style.*

You will no doubt have noticed that in this book we don't apply all the rules for formal writing that we're suggesting for you. This was a conscious decision. Before we started, we decided that because we spend much of our working life with students, we should try to develop a similar relationship with you, our readers, as we have with the students we teach. We hope and believe that there is a friendly and informal atmosphere in our lectures, and we have therefore adopted a similar style in the book, but on other occasions, when it's more appropriate, we write in a more distant and formal style.

We've stressed 'writing', as there are major differences between the way in which we use the language in writing and the way in which we speak, as we saw in the passages above. We'll analyse these differences more closely in considering the spoken language (see pages 112–14), but it's important now to recognize that 'writing as I speak' is a difficult and unsatisfactory way of communicating.

When we speak, we use techniques which aren't available to the writer. Even a simple expression such as 'thank you' can be spoken in ways which suggest genuine gratitude, sarcasm, irritation at being kept waiting, condescension, disregard and no doubt many other states of mind. The meaning depends heavily on the tone used and the emphasis given. Tone and emphasis aren't as obvious in writing; we need to add other words, describe our meaning more fully or, if absolutely necessary, use artificial means such as underlining.

For these reasons, and others such as body language (see pages 141–5), we convey our meaning more easily in speech than in writing: our grammar can become careless, we can jump from one sentence to another without completing the first, we can repeat details that we want to stress, and generally speaking it doesn't greatly matter. In writing, we have to express our meaning as precisely and concisely as possible, although we have one obvious advantage in that our readers can reread something if they didn't understand it the first time, although if they have to do this too often, they may well give up in disgust.

Good writing in this context, then, involves using all the tools available in an accurate way in order to help and encourage our readers; we must keep both the needs of our readers and the purpose for which we're writing in mind. Our primary tools are words and sentence structure, and each will be discussed in turn.

▶ Words

Words: formal and informal

Earlier in this chapter, we commented that university writing is generally formal and this consideration affects our choice of words. Some words are in their nature 'chatty', and not appropriate to formal writing. We might (perhaps!) say:

> Francis Bacon was such a dry old stick that he couldn't ever have written Shakespeare's plays. Christopher Marlowe was really cool, but he was wiped out far too soon.

It's unlikely we'd write such expressions. Of course, it's an extreme example, but it's dangerously easy to make notes in the way in which we think through the information, and then, perhaps because of shortage of time, to transfer casual or colloquial expressions into an essay. It isn't acceptable, by the way, to put an unsuitable word in quotation marks, as we did with the word 'chatty', above: it simply says to the reader that you couldn't be bothered to find a better word (such as 'conversational').

You will have noticed that the example includes the abbreviation *couldn't*; this is very informal, and so appropriate in speech or casual writing, but not in the style we're describing. Always spell out such expressions: use *do not* rather than *don't*, *shall not* rather than *shan't*, *it is* or *it has* rather than *it's*. The abbreviations, as we noticed earlier, aren't used in the formal academic style.

Formal writing tries to be as precise as possible. Avoid expressions such as *a lot of*, *quite*, *fairly*, *comparatively often* (compared to what?), which give very little information to the reader. If you want to show how often Shakespeare uses the word 'nothing' in *King Lear*, use a Shakespeare concordance, or count them!

Words: jargon

Some words are part of your academic jargon, such as terms which you use regularly in your writing, but which are less common in daily communication. You can't avoid such expressions, and shouldn't try, but make sure that you use them accurately. An example which students often choose is the word 'dramatic', as in 'Ibsen used dramatic language.' Of course he did – he was a playwright! The writer usually means something like 'shocking language', which is a much more precise way of describing Ibsen's writing.

There is, however, a different kind of jargon which you should always try to avoid. It tends to be wordy, it's probably a cliché, and it will irritate your readers. The most famous example is *at this present moment in time*, meaning *now*, but other expressions become fashionable and are then overused in a similar way. *Basically*, for example, can have a useful meaning ('this is basically a simple question, but has been made to sound complicated . . . '), but it is often used carelessly, in much the same way as 'actually' ('this is actually the right style' means no more than 'this is the right style').

Words to be used with care

Words are often used carelessly, in spite of the fact that they should carry the writer's meaning. We'll look at a few examples which are frequently found in student writing; there are many more, of course, but we'd like to alert you to a few that we find commonly misused:

- then
- only
- less/fewer
- amount/number
- greater part/majority
- disinterested/uninterested
- infer/imply
- fortunately/fortuitously.

Then is often added to a sentence in a meaningless way; if it's overused, it can produce boring writing, for example:

> Expenditure on Poor Relief in the UK rose between 1783 and 1833, then it fell until 1843, then it rose again until 1863 and then . . .

and so on! The repeated use of 'then' adds nothing to the meaning, and has a dulling effect on the whole passage.

A far more dangerous word is *only*. This little word influences the nearest word or expression, and as a result its position can change the meaning of the whole sentence:

> This book is available to order and for this term will cost twenty pounds.

If we add *only* to any point of the sentence, we will change the meaning: 'this book only . . .' means that no other book is in this category; 'is available only to order' means that it *has* to be ordered; 'for this term only' means that the price will change after this term; 'will cost only twenty pounds' suggests that it's cheap at the price. If *only* is placed carelessly in a sentence, the whole message can be distorted; it must be kept close to the words it influences.

There is one other problem with 'only', and that is its use in casual speech to mean 'but', as in:

> I'd like to go, only I don't think I can spare the time.

As long as we use the word in this way only when we're speaking, it isn't likely to cause misunderstanding, but it should never be used in writing.

Groups of words can become confused and so cause misunderstanding. Three awkward combinations are *less/fewer*, *amount/number* and *greater part/majority*. In each case, the first expression (*less*, *amount*, *greater part*) is used to describe variation in one single object or idea, as in:

> There was less work involved than I expected.

> The amount of material available was surprisingly small.

> The greater part of the time was spent in preparation.

The second expression in each case (*fewer*, *number*, *majority*) is used when there are several objects or ideas involved, as in:

> There are fewer books on the subject than I expected.

> The number of students studying languages has declined.

> A majority of those interviewed wanted to work in the financial sector.

Interestingly, we can think of *less* as qualitative (qualifying the amount of work) and *fewer* as quantitative (a measure of the number of books). The distinction between these words should be kept in mind, as the meaning of the sentence might depend on their accurate use: the distinction between *less important qualifications* and *fewer important qualifications* could be critical!

Some pairs of words are misused even by people who should know better. We've chosen three examples to represent this category, and we suggest that you are precise in using these words and look out for other examples so that you can use them correctly as well.

If you are *disinterested*, you are impartial, you have no particular prejudice about the subject. This is, we hope, how you approach each new topic in your course: you will wait until you've looked at it before starting to make up your mind. On the other hand, we hope that you will never be *uninterested*, as this means that you have no interest in the topic, that you're almost bored by it.

Infer and imply are frequently confused. You might think of them as the opposite ends of a telephone conversation: you *imply* that you might be free to go out in the evening, and your friend, listening, *infers* that you've almost finished the essay you're writing. If you imply, you suggest something; if the hint is picked up, the other person has inferred your meaning.

One more common confusion is between fortunate and fortuitous. A *fortunate* happening is a lucky one, which works out well for the people concerned. If something happens *fortuitously*, it happens by accident. It was probably fortuitous that Othello should have had Iago as his lieutenant, but nobody could claim that it was fortunate for either of them!

As we've said, there are many such easily confused words, but your job as a student is to write precisely. In these and all cases, you need to choose the correct word and not be misled by the mistakes you sometimes see in print.

> *Key point: choose your words with care so that they accurately reflect your meaning.*

Words: American usage

Different countries that have English as their first language use it slightly differently: inevitably, the language has developed in each country in line with the culture and history. We and North Americans may both speak English, but in small ways there are variations in our usage. This isn't generally very important, except that many computers use American spellchecks and grammar checks, and we need to be sure which form of the language we're actually producing.

In English, we sometimes have a difference of spelling to show the use of a word: *practice* with a 'c' is a noun while *practise* with an 's' is a verb. This *c/s* distinction isn't always made in the same way in American English, which tends to use the 's' form more freely (our *defence* is *defense* in American). There are too many differences to be discussed here, but you will notice that in English, as opposed to American, *program* refers specifically to a computer program while other kinds of programme, for instance at a theatre, are still spelt in the traditional way, with 'mme'. If you use American English for some reason, you will need to be consistent: *centre* will be written as *center*, *colour* as *color* and *travelling* as *traveling*. Generally, it's better to keep to the form of the language which is natural to you. It doesn't matter whether you spell words such as *organise* in this way or as *organize*, but again it is important to be consistent.

You may find that the grammar check on your computer highlights your use of *which* in a sentence such as 'These books, which I borrowed from the library, are very heavy.' The Americans use 'that' where we would tend to use 'which'; ignore the prompting of the computer and follow your own instincts.

Words: singulars and plurals

Spelling is always a problem in English: words come into the language from many sources, and so are formed in different ways. For example, Latin 'a' endings become 'ae' in the plural, so that *antenna* becomes *antennae*. Words which have been derived from Greek often end in 'on' in the singular and 'a' in the plural, such as *criterion, criteria* and *phenomenon, phenomena*. Spelling rules themselves are often cumbersome and hard to remember, or have so many exceptions that it hardly seems to be worth the effort; perhaps the old saying 'i before e except after c, as long as the sound is ee' is one of the few which are sufficiently useful to be learnt.

Words can change their usage as time passes. *Data* is technically a plural word (singular: *datum*), but it's often used as a collective singular nowadays. You will probably feel that you should keep to the classical plural use, but whichever decision you make, be consistent. Other words in the same form, such as *media* (singular: *medium*), are often mistakenly used as singular, perhaps on the analogy of data, but this is still viewed as incorrect.

Words: new developments

Languages aren't static: they change in response to many kinds of influence, and they expand with the development of new ideas and technology. As a result, you may find yourself unsure about the suitability, or the form, of new expressions. After all, the word *mouse* used to make people think first of a small furry animal! Sometimes adjectives are used as nouns: people will speak of a *floppy*, or a *remote*. Words are often abbreviated, such as *quote* for *quotation*, and nouns are also used as verbs, as in *tasking* someone with a piece of work. Be aware that words and expressions change their meaning and notice examples as you read, but for the purposes of your academic study, use the conventional forms, that is, *quotation* in full. Don't try to start a new fashion in the use of words, and be sensitive to the very fine distinctions between what is modern and what is conventional. Don't assume that new forms are necessarily acceptable, and if in doubt, check.

Some new inventions are both ugly and unnecessary. A student recently wrote:

This allows reuseability and upgradeability.

which is, in its way, perfectly clear, although it sounds ugly and uses abstract nouns when verbs would be more natural. It's just as easy, and far more readable, to write:

This allows [the product] to be reused and upgraded.

> *Key point: be alert to changes in the meaning and use of words, but, in academic writing, follow convention.*

▶ Punctuation

Before we move on from words to sentences, it's worth looking at the main forms of punctuation as they are used in formal writing. Accuracy is just as important here, for poor punctuation can affect the reading, making comprehension difficult or creating ambiguity. Good punctuation, on the other hand, guides the reader through the information and adds considerably to the ease and pleasure of reading.

We use much less punctuation than we did in the past. This is partly the effect of word processing – saving keystrokes means saving time and therefore money – and partly a desire to simplify the language. Sometimes this doesn't matter; for example, whether we indent paragraphs or punctuate addresses is no more than a matter of taste or convention. At other times, the punctuation is critical to the meaning, and to leave it out is a crime against the accurate transmission of information and ideas.

In this section, some of the most common types of punctuation are described, with a short example in each case, and a comment on any particular problems with usage. You will find help with more complex questions of punctuation style in the MHRA *Style Book* which we mentioned in writing about references. There will probably be a copy in your department and certainly in your library.

Full stops

Full stops are one of the simplest and clearest forms of punctuation. They appear at the end of a sentence (for the definition of a sentence, see page 88), and are followed by a capital letter at the start of the first word of the next sentence.

Full stops used to appear in abbreviations, but do so more rarely nowadays. Most people write *etc* and *eg* without full stops, but you would be wise to check whether this is acceptable in your writing. In continuous prose, such as an essay or dissertation as opposed to notes, it's better style to avoid eg and write *for example* in full. The same applies to ie: use *that is*.

There is, however, a rule for using a full stop in other abbreviations: if the abbreviation ends with the last letter of the full word, there is no full stop; if it doesn't, there is. Following this rule, the word Doctor can be abbreviated as Dr with no full stop, while Professor can be abbreviated as Prof. with a full stop.

Colons and semi-colons

Colons and semi-colons are different pieces of punctuation, but as they are often confused, it makes sense to treat them together. A major use of the full colon (:) is to introduce a list, whether it is written down the page or, if it's short, along the line. So we may write:

Three well-known composers died in 1934: Delius, Elgar and Holst.

A longer list which is written down the page is treated in the same way, except that it probably won't have internal punctuation such as commas; a final full stop is useful in clearly identifying the end of the list, especially if it coincides with the foot of the page. The example which follows shows how the list may be set out and punctuated:

The following source material is available for this project:

- court reports
- primary texts
- secondary texts.

If any of the items in a list are themselves long enough to run onto a second line, use the colon to introduce the list, and then semi-colons to help the reader to identify the end of each point, as in:

The following source material is available to you for use in this project:

- court reports, particularly probate reports;
- primary texts, and especially the ones to be found on the Module 2 reading list;
- secondary texts, although those which were published prior to the 1981 legislation mentioned in the lecture will be of little use.

Follow this same pattern if each item in a list is itself a full sentence, but use the normal full stop at the end of each.

We've dealt with lists in some detail because they are very useful to the writer: it's easier to think your way clearly through the information if you use a list rather than a long paragraph, and it's certainly easier for the reader to absorb information in this form. It's useful to notice, too, that the items in a list can have bullet points, as in the examples, or may be numbered or lettered, if their order is important.

Another important way in which you are likely to use a colon in your writing is as the introduction to a quotation. You will notice that all the indented examples in this book have been introduced by colons; every time that you quote a sufficiently long passage, that is, a line or more in length of print, set it out in this way and use a colon. (See also the note on references, pages 29–30.)

There is yet another use of the colon which will be very useful to you. A colon is used when the first part of a sentence is developed and amplified in the second. So we may write:

> I do not agree with the writer: the issue is clearly more important than he suggests.

In this example, the disagreement stated in the first part of the sentence is amplified in the second. Another example might be:

> There are two possible positions to take about the death penalty: people are strongly in favour or horrified at the very idea.

The 'two possible positions' of the first part of the sentence are defined more fully in the second part. Such a use of the colon is likely to occur quite often in an essay which discusses opposing attitudes to a moral or philosophical question.

Semi-colons are very strong punctuation – almost as powerful as, and sometimes an alternative to, a full stop. They should therefore be used sparingly. If two ideas are closely linked, by a logical connection or perhaps a contrast, and they would normally be written as two separate grammatical sentences, a semi-colon can be used to bring them together. They become two equal parts of one sentence (there's no capital letter after a semi-colon), and the connection between them is emphasized, as in the following example:

> Ancient Greece is considered to have been the birthplace of democracy; its political system, however, was not without fault.

Commas

Commas are the hardest punctuation to discuss, as their use often depends on the sensitivity of the writer rather than on hard and fast rules. There are, however, occasions when a comma is essential if the reader is to understand the sense of the sentence. If we write:

> The sentences which I've written under examination conditions are confused and ungrammatical.

we're saying that of all the sentences available, those which I've written under examination conditions are distinguished from the others by being confused and ungrammatical. If, on the other hand, we put commas round the words 'which I've written under examination conditions', we link these words to 'the sentences'; we are in fact describing all these sentences. So if we write:

> The sentences, which I've written under examination conditions, are confused and ungrammatical.

we're saying that all the sentences we're talking about were written under examination conditions and therefore had the undesirable features.

The presence or absence of commas can change the meaning in more subtle ways, as in the following:

> To an extent, 1915 was a year of muddle and adjustment. Only the following year after the catastrophe of the first day of the Battle of the Somme in 1916 were lessons learnt.

This suggests that after the muddle of 1915, there was the Battle of the Somme in 1916, and lessons were learnt in the following year, 1917. Correctly used commas change this to:

> To an extent, 1915 was a year of muddle and adjustment. Only the following year, after the catastrophe of the first day of the Battle of the Somme in 1916, were lessons learnt.

We now know that the lessons were learnt the year after 1915, that is, the year of the Battle of the Somme in 1916. The implications of the dates given in the sentence are changed by the commas.

You will probably have noticed that introductory expressions often take a comma, to show that they are a comment on the sentence that follows rather than a major part of it: *in this case*, *as you see*, are in this category. Other 'comment' expressions often found in the middle of a sentence also have commas round them, such as *that is*, or *on the other hand*.

Commas are also used to add information which is said to be 'in apposition', that is, an extra piece of information added to words which themselves form a major part of the sentence. So we can write:

> Professor Jones, head of the history department, has written a new book.

In this case we are adding information about Professor Jones immediately after his name is mentioned. Another example might be:

> The student email system, installed a few years ago, has already proved its worth.

In each case, the extra description ('head of the history department' and 'installed a few years ago') is enclosed by commas; you will notice that if you read these sentences aloud, you will naturally pause in the places marked by the commas.

This is the point at which the discussion of commas becomes less precise, and the writer's feeling for the flow of the language takes over. Most fairly long sentences (perhaps more than about 25 words, although it's impossible to be precise) have a break built into them; when you read them out loud, you will probably pause and perhaps take a breath at these places. In writing, a comma marks the pause. Probably the easiest way to find out where to put such commas is to read the sentence aloud and notice where your voice wants to pause. This isn't an infallible guide, but it's a useful one all the same.

Later in this chapter (see pages 88–9), we discuss how long a sentence should be and the problems of overlong sentences, but it's worth stressing here how useful commas are in guiding the reader through the text, showing how sections of a sentence belong together and are separated from other developments of the idea. You have just seen this process in action: my previous sentence contained 53 words, which means that it's rather long. It contains:

- introductory words (Later in this chapter)
- a reference in brackets (see pages 88–9)
- an informative section (we discuss . . . overlong sentences)
- a second informative section (but it's worth stressing . . . through the text)
- a development of the ideas (showing how . . . the idea).

It would be difficult to read and absorb so much information in one sentence if it weren't for the commas, and you will notice how they occur at each transition point within the information.

In your own reading, see how such commas help the flow, but be careful in your writing not to put commas where they interrupt the flow, as in:

> Theatres, and other places of entertainment were closed during the English Civil War in the seventeenth century.

If you read this sentence aloud, you are unlikely to pause only after 'theatres'. You might read the whole sentence without a break as it isn't very long, or you might pause twice:

> Theatres, and other places of entertainment, were closed during the English Civil War in the seventeenth century.

The two pauses are now shown by the two commas.

Apostrophes

Of all the punctuation in the English language, it's probably fair to say that the apostrophe causes most difficulty – so much so, that some people simply ignore it altogether, as George Bernard Shaw did many years ago. This is not sensible, however, as the apostrophe can show whether a word is singular or plural, and this may be important to the meaning. Its absence also makes the text look casual and perhaps careless; if the student hasn't bothered to use apostrophes, perhaps it's because he or she has a poor grasp of the language as a whole.

Apostrophes aren't as bad as they're painted, once you grasp the principles. One of their uses is to show where a letter or letters have been omitted, for example *don't*, *can't*, *wouldn't*. The good news is that in formal writing such expressions should always be written out in full, as *do not*, *cannot*, *would not*, and so there is no need for an apostrophe at all.

This is true even in the most contentious case of all: *it's*. This means *it is*, or *it has*, as in 'it's time to hand in the assignment' or 'it's been a long term', and under no other circumstances does the word ever have an apostrophe. If you are writing a formal document like a dissertation, write out *it is* or *it has* in full.

The confusion is caused partly by the other use of the apostrophe, which is to show possession. This is the case in which the singular or the plural is so important: 'the student's failure' (one student has failed) needs to be carefully distinguished from 'the students' failure' (more than one student has failed). Only the position of the apostrophe will reveal the difference of meaning.

If you remember these principles, you won't go wrong with the apostrophe. One of the two most depressing sights for a lecturer (we speak from years of experience) is to see ordinary plural words with apostrophes just because they end in *s*, even though there is no suggestion of a letter omitted or of possession – and the other is to see the word 'its' with an inappropriate apostrophe!

Hyphens

As with commas, so with hyphens: we use fewer that we used to, and this often causes no problem at all. However, we can't dispense with hyphens altogether, partly because they can affect the meaning and partly because they can help the reader to understand easily and quickly what we mean.

A few examples will show how the use of a hyphen aids the reading:

> a cross-section of students
> pro-Communist activity
> self-evidently true

Hyphens can also tell the reader how to understand the phrase in which they occur. 'A cross bearer' is different from 'a cross-bearer', and 'twenty five year cycles' from 'twenty-five year cycles'. We read 'the nineteenth century' differently from 'a nineteenth-century politician' because, in the latter, the hyphen tells us that 'nineteenth-century' is an adjectival phrase in which the words that are hyphenated belong together.

Brackets

On the whole, brackets are best reserved for information which isn't an integral part of the sentence, as in the following examples (*see Figure 3.1*) or (*see Appendix A*), and in abbreviations. The traditional way of introducing an abbreviation is by writing the term out in full on the first occasion on which it's used, and putting the abbreviation in brackets immediately afterwards. After this, the abbreviation can be used by itself as in the following example:

The *Oxford English Dictionary* (*OED*) has been cited throughout the dissertation.

There is an entirely different use of brackets which will be useful to you in writing a dissertation or similar document. Square brackets are sometimes used in quotations, when, in order to make the words quoted understandable, you need to add something to the exact words you are quoting. This happened earlier in this chapter, when we were discussing the ugliness of some modern word forms. We quoted the words 'reusability and upgradeability', and showed how the idea could be conveyed in better style as:

This allowed [the product] to be reused and upgraded.

We added the words 'the product' to make sense of the new sentence, but put them in square brackets to show that they were our words and not the writer's.

You may find that as you use quotations, you often need to add a word or two in square brackets in order to make sense, as in:

T S Eliot writes that in the mind of the poet [in this case, John Donne] experiences are always forming new wholes.

Other punctuation

Other forms of punctuation, such as exclamation marks and question marks, are used comparatively rarely in formal writing. Indeed, if you find that you are using them often, you may need to think again about your style. It's also a good idea to use the dash sparingly as punctuation; a pair of dashes can occasionally take the place of a pair of commas, but the single dash, sometimes used instead of a colon, is too informal for academic writing.

As we suggested earlier, a useful check on your punctuation is to read a passage of your writing out loud; if you find that you want to pause at exactly the point at which you've used punctuation, you are probably right, but if your voice is constantly stumbling over oddly placed commas or stops, you need to rethink what you are writing.

Key point: use punctuation correctly to clarify your meaning, give emphasis and guide the reader through the information.

▶ Sentences

Before we discuss how sentences can be misformed and misused, we
need to stress that a sentence must make sense by itself; we might not
fully understand it without its context, but we should see that it contains
a complete message. This means that it must contain a main verb, one
which makes sense. If we say 'Jane *read* the book', the verb 'read'
makes sense, as does 'Jane *was reading* the book'. However, 'Jane *reading* the book' doesn't make sense, as 'reading' by itself can't be a main
verb. If we remember that, it's obvious that the following aren't
sentences:

> With reference to the previous example.
> For the following reasons.
> As detailed below.
> Looking at both sides of the question.

The same criterion of complete sense applies if we try to use
a subordinate clause by itself. It will probably begin with a word that
shows a logical link to something else, as in these examples:

> As we saw earlier.
> Whenever the character appears.
> However we look at the problem.

It's obvious that none of these makes sense by itself: they all need to be
completed by other information which contains a main verb, such as:

> As we saw earlier, apostrophes aren't as difficult to use as people think.
> Whenever the character appears, the audience feels that the mood
> of the play changes.
> However we look at the problem, there is no easy solution.

In formal writing, we must always write in sentences which are
complete and correct; if we're simply writing notes, we can, of course,
write incomplete messages, as long as we're sure that we'll understand
them later, but as soon as we're writing for other people to read, we must
be sure that our sentences will stand by themselves.

Sentence length
A sentence can be too long for easy reading for two different but related
reasons. It may contain too many words or too many ideas. Either fault
causes problems for the reader. When we read difficult information, we

instinctively look out for a full stop, in the knowledge that we can pause at that point, reread if we have to, think about the implications of what we've read, or even ask advice if it seems appropriate. If we find that we're looking over several lines of print with no obvious place to pause, we start to panic, and either add our own full stop, not necessarily in the right place, or give up on the sentence and move on, hoping that all will become clear later.

For this reason, sentence length needs to be under the writer's control. Good style involves variety in the length of sentences, some sentences being short and therefore emphatic, and others, because they contain more complex thought, being longer. However, none should be long simply because the writer is wandering from one point to the next without considering the overall shape of the sentence, as in this example:

> There are many forms of stanza available to the poet, from the simple couplet through the tercet with its single rhyme over three lines, the Spenserian stanza which has nine lines, to the fourteen-line sonnet or even the canto, which is a section of a long narrative poem.

Rambling, overlong sentences are far too common in student writing. They are not only difficult to assimilate; they often include grammatical mistakes and ambiguity which compound the problems for the reader. If you keep your sentences reasonably short, but allow for some variation of length, you are likely to write more accurately as well as in a more readable way.

As a test of your writing, look back at an essay you wrote a few months ago, and count the number of words in the sentences. If you have many of 50 or more words, decide whether this is justified by the argument or whether you have simply included far more ideas than one sentence should be asked to carry.

Sentence structure

Even in a comparatively short sentence, it's generally true that the first few words make more impact on the reader than later words. For this reason, it's generally a good idea to put the main point of a sentence at the beginning. We said 'generally', as there are times when you delib-erately don't want to stress a particular point, or when you might choose to give the reader a surprise by withholding a major idea until the end of a sentence. Such occasions are rare; mostly, we know which point we want to stress and will therefore put it first. The difference of impact can be seen in the following examples:

> The prime minister made an interesting speech during what was otherwise an uneventful conference.

This construction stresses the prime minister's speech, while:

> During an otherwise uneventful conference, the prime minister made an interesting speech.

stresses the uneventful conference.

Sentences sometimes begin in one construction and change to another halfway through, because the writer hasn't thought through the message before beginning to write. Two typical examples are:

> This method has both advantages as well as disadvantages.
> The reason for the failure of the seminar was because the students had failed to prepare adequately.

The first writer could have said 'both advantages and disadvantages', or 'advantages as well as disadvantages', but trying to say both at once is clumsy as well as ungrammatical; the second could have said either 'the reason that the seminar failed was that...' or 'the seminar failed because...'. Whichever construction is chosen, it must be used consistently.

Key point: keep the length and structure of sentences under your control.

Infinitives, split and otherwise

The infinitive of the verb is its name: we identify the verb 'to be' or 'to read' or 'to think' by using the 'to' form. The two words that make up the infinitive (for example, 'to' and 'read') belong together, and on the whole it's bad style to split them by putting other words in between. So 'to thoroughly read' should be written as 'to read thoroughly'. However, we occasionally want to stress the word that describes the verb (called an adverb), and in this case, we can be forgiven for putting it between the parts of the infinitive, provided that we do this very rarely, and for a clear purpose. So we could accept 'to apprehensively read' (expecting to find the book impossibly difficult) if the writer is deliberately trying to take us aback by the use of the word 'apprehensively'. The rule is probably: don't split an infinitive by accident.

Interestingly, a sentence that begins with the infinitive of the verb is usually awkward to read, and better turned round, as in:

> To ensure that the results are valid, the researchers need to choose their data carefully.

which would be more logically ordered as:

> The researchers need to choose their data carefully in order to ensure that the results are valid.

Singular and plural agreement

If the subject of the verb is singular, the form of the verb must also be singular; in the same way, a plural subject must be followed by a plural verb. Difficulties often arise when there are several words between the subject and the verb, as in:

> Each of the options, regardless of recent student demonstrations, are to be considered next week.

This is wrong: the subject is 'each', which is singular (not the plural 'options'), and the verb must agree, as in:

> Each of the options, regardless of recent student demonstrations, is to be considered next week.

Beginnings of sentences

The first few words of a sentence, as we've said, have more emphasis than what follows. This impact is lost if too many sentences start in the same way. A student trying to explain how a survey had been carried out, might write sentences which begin:

> First, I . . . Then I . . . Then I . . . Finally I . . .

This is boring to read. Try to vary the beginnings of sentences, so that the reader's attention is held.

We've highlighted some common mistakes and, we hope, given you some ideas for writing effective sentences. Read critically, especially textbooks by acknowledged experts in your field of study, and you will see ways of expressing complex thoughts clearly and succinctly for your readers.

▶ Paragraphs

Essentially, a paragraph contains a single theme or unit of an argument; when you get to the end of this line of argument, close the paragraph. However, we may sometimes have too much material which belongs together, or we may feel that, for the sake of the reader, we need to break up the text. Lists are described elsewhere (see pages 81–2); they can be a more convenient way to handle information than long paragraphs.

Apply the same test to paragraphs as you did earlier to sentences: count them in a typical essay, and you should find some variety in their length. If too many are long, a page or more, ask why and decide whether they are justified by the content.

As we move from one paragraph to the next, we can use connecting words or phrases to show the relationship of the new paragraph to the old: 'At the same time...', 'On the other hand...', 'Under such circumstances...' are typical of these logical links; apart from their work in connecting pieces of text, they guide the reader towards what follows.

> *Key point: check the length of your paragraphs, and consider whether a list would be better than an overlong paragraph.*

▶ Active or passive?

There is no clear answer to the decision about whether to use the active or the passive voice; as so often in writing, it depends on the effect you want to create. We will start with a small example to illustrate both ways of writing:

> Susan studied both books.

This is the active form: Susan is the subject of the verb 'studied', and 'both books' is the object. The words are given in the most common order. If we turn the sentence round to make the object into the subject, as in:

> Both books were studied by Susan.

we have made the sentence passive. You will notice straightaway that even in such a little example, the active form is shorter and more direct; it makes a bigger impact. This is nearly always the case. There is also a change of emphasis: in the active version, Susan gets the stress, while in the passive form, the books are at the beginning of the sentence and so get more emphasis.

In the same way, we might say:

> Shakespeare wrote one hundred and twenty sonnets.

or

> One hundred and twenty sonnets were written by Shakespeare.

depending on whether the poet or the number is more important in the context.

Both ways of writing are well-named: the active stresses the doer, and is brief and direct; the passive puts the emphasis on the object, and is longer and gentler in its effect. The choice is yours, but be aware of the difference of impact that results from your decision.

> *Key point: choose the active or the passive in order to create a particular effect in your writing.*

▶ Inclusive language

In the past, most people wrote as if the readership were exclusively male, as in:

> The reader would have expected a different result if he had had prior knowledge of the evidence presented.

This is no longer acceptable. Nevertheless, you will want to avoid the cumbersome 'he or she' as far as you can, although, as we have found in writing this book, it's sometimes difficult to do so. On the whole, the plural will solve the problem ('Readers would expect ... if they ... '); sometimes using the passive will help, or restructuring the sentence, but if occasionally you are forced to use 'he or she', nobody is likely to query it, as, after all, you are showing your awareness of the need to use inclusive language.

> *Key point: don't offend your readers by using sexist language.*

▶ Listening to language

We can tell a great deal about language by hearing it. From time to time, choose a paragraph which you wrote a few days ago, and try to read it aloud. You will soon notice if your punctuation is in the wrong place, if you've repeated words in an awkward way (good style doesn't allow repetition of a word within a line or two, unless the word is so specific in meaning that there's no alternative), your sentence is so long that you run out of breath or your voice doesn't know where to go next. It's much easier to hear these problems than to see them on the page. If it's easy to read what you've written, and it sounds as if it flows well, you have the enormous advantage of being able to write in a way which will attract your readers. As we said earlier in this chapter, good writing is always appropriate to the readers and the occasion.

Part Three
Speaking Skills

5 Small-group Presentations

'We consider it vital to your education and future career prospects to develop your oral, as well as written, skills.' In this part of our book, we will be looking at the oral skills highlighted in this quotation, taken from the brochure of a university arts department. The statement it makes is correct: at some point or points during your course, you will have to lead a seminar or discussion or make a presentation. When you go to a job interview, you may find that you have to make a presentation as part of the selection process; when you are launched into your career, you may well find that you are expected, without further training, to talk to groups of people as part of your job or on behalf of your organization. Talking to an audience is becoming more and more important, both socially and academically.

As you will see, we've divided this subject, slightly artificially, into small-group presentations and formal presentations. Of course you may speak formally to a few people or lead a discussion with a large group, but our distinction is a useful one in allowing us to consider the range of 'talking' experiences you're likely to meet during your course. Chapter 7, the third chapter dealing with speaking, is called 'Delivery and Non-verbal Communication'; it discusses those skills which underlie any presentation, speaking effectively and using body language to reinforce your message. You may wish to read that chapter straight after this one if you need immediate advice about giving a seminar paper.

So let's first define some terms. By seminar, we mean a talk and discussion on a prepared topic, which is likely to involve about a dozen people; a tutorial (or supervision) is a discussion based on the return of marked work, normally involving the tutor and one or two students (generally not more than four). A presentation is a formal talk given by one or more people to an audience; the talk itself is likely to be quite short, commonly ten or fifteen minutes, followed by questions and answers. You may find that your institution uses these terms differently, but the forms will almost certainly be these. In this chapter, we'll look at seminars, including the discussion element, and tutorials, while more formal presentations will be discussed in detail in the next chapter. Of course, there is likely to be some overlap between the different forms.

▶ Seminars

You almost certainly won't have met seminars at school or college, or at work, and so they will be a new experience in which you'll probably be involved very early in your course. You may be asked to lead a seminar about once a term, but you'll be a participant much more frequently, usually once a week. There are different types of seminar, which we'll look at in turn, but each will involve at least one tutor and up to about a dozen students, and will last for one class, that is, about fifty minutes.

General seminars
In some ways, a general seminar is a bit like an informal lecture, in that the session is led by the tutor, but with students commenting and asking questions. There is one golden rule about such occasions: everybody, and that includes you, must be prepared. The session will be successful only if you and the other students have read the text, or thought about and read round the subject, beforehand. The tutor will introduce the topic, speaking for perhaps ten or fifteen minutes to get you going, and then there will be a pause. If nobody has anything to say, the silence gets embarrassing. If the tutor ends up by having to do all the talking, including asking and answering all the questions, he or she will be fed up and you will have lost a valuable opportunity to think round the ideas, try out a different point of view, follow up something that interests you, or just have the experience of speaking to a group. If all you do is ask a question, you have contributed, and this will encourage you to speak at more length in future, perhaps to lead a seminar later in the term (see the next section on student-led seminars).

Your great fear is probably that you might look foolish. It's bad if the tutor thinks you're stupid, but much worse if your colleagues do too, and this often inhibits students, especially early on in the course. Such fear sometimes makes people sound more aggressive than they intended, and so it's wise to think briefly about how you word your question – 'I wonder whether . . .' is a safer introduction than 'I think you're wrong'.

It would be good if we could say that all lecturers are totally supportive of their students if they genuinely make an attempt to contribute, but of course this isn't so; nevertheless, the great majority are so pleased that you've tried to join in, even if you've got it wrong, that they will show their appreciation as they gently correct you. Your colleagues are likely to be grateful to you for starting the discussion, so you have little to lose.

> *Key point: think about the seminar subject in advance, and be ready to participate, even if it's just to ask a question.*

Student-led seminars

Sooner or later, you'll find yourself having to lead a seminar. This may primarily involve leading a discussion after giving a short introduction to the topic; you may be asked to do this in company with another student or by yourself. On the other hand, you may be asked to give a seminar paper, that is, to present a topic at length (perhaps for as much as half an hour) and then lead a discussion. This is in some ways similar to the formal presentation discussed in the next chapter, and so if you have to present a seminar paper, you might want to read that chapter as well as this one; you will certainly need the information on delivering your paper, which you will find in Chapter 7.

In any case, planning and preparation are essential. You will almost certainly be given your topic, but in a form which is too wide in scope for a short discussion. You'll need to read as much background as you can, using any bibliography you've been given, to see how the subject can be approached in a way which will not get out of hand. We've already looked at some of the implications of this in the section on dissertation planning, but it's worth saying again that the best work has the narrowest base: say something about a very small topic, rather than gloss over a great deal in general terms.

Of course, your initial reading will need to be as wide as possible in the time available. Time is an important consideration. You may be given your topic at the beginning of term, or even at the end of the previous term, so that you have plenty of time for reading. On the other hand, you may be told to prepare the seminar for the following week, in which case you will have less time for reading, but the time that is available must be sensibly allocated. Don't leave all your preparation until the day before the seminar, as you will then have no opportunity either for adequate reading or assessing the information you have found. Incidentally, conscientious students sometimes fall into this trap by being too scared to start work: they seem to think that if they ignore the problem, it will go away. Alas, it won't, and they are making even greater problems for themselves in the end.

Whichever form your seminar is going to take, remember that you are primarily talking to people. We said earlier (page 13) that human beings are poor listeners, and so it's important not to overload them with detail. You need a clear structure in which the main points you want to make stand out in a way that can be easily assimilated; make sure that you have backup information, so that if your tutor asks why you made a particular decision, you can explain, but don't try to give a source for everything you say while you are talking.

> *Key point: if you are leading a seminar, read as widely as time allows, and structure your ideas. Don't overwhelm your audience with detail.*

There is one point you should clarify straightaway. Is any of your material to be handed in for marking? If so, and if you have notes to speak from, will they be acceptable? If you have a full script, it will be in a less formal style if you are speaking from it than if it were intended just to be read (see pages 71–3 for a more detailed discussion of this point). Is this acceptable, or will you need to rewrite it in more formal essay style? Unless you have already been told, clarify these questions with your tutor before you start work.

In order to show how material can be organized for each type of student-led seminar, we will use an example from a first-year philosophy course. The students have been studying the work of the twentieth-century philosopher Peter Singer. The question given to one of the class, Susan Phillips, is as follows:

> What are Singer's views on the killing of animals? How far do you agree with them?

(NB: both the discussion and the seminar paper which follow have been simplified and shortened for the purpose of this chapter.)

Susan has to lead a discussion on this topic, starting with an introduction of five to seven minutes. The question clearly has two parts, and it seems sensible to spend most of the introduction time explaining Singer's views. This allows Susan the chance to identify the parts of Singer's work that she wants to deal with in the very short time available, and also ensures that other students will be able to find something to say, even if they haven't done the required reading.

So Susan will start with Singer's suggestion that killing a person may be 'more seriously wrong' than killing a non-person, and with his definition of 'person'. She realizes that it isn't easy to absorb a definition just by hearing it, and so she decides that she will write the definition on the board before the class starts, but reveal it by turning the board at the appropriate point, allowing the class a brief time in which to read it or copy it down (see pages 127–8). She will then add that the definition of 'a self-conscious being' applies to chimpanzees, perhaps even more than to newborn human infants. This is something the class might like to discuss. Are there human non-persons? How far are we prejudiced about animals by conditioning, for example, farm animals, wild animals, pets? How far are we affected by cruelty in the killing?

There are plenty of ideas here to generate discussion, and Susan has used up most of her introductory time. The class can take over, with guidance as necessary from the tutor. When the discussion starts to peter out, Susan moves to a new aspect, that of human beings eating meat. How far are the animals we eat 'conscious' or 'self-conscious'? Are the struggles of trapped animals just reflexes, or do they show an awareness of pain? Do we have to kill for food, and do we try to avoid knowing about the process of killing for food? Susan has scarcely introduced these ideas when a couple of vegetarians in the class jump in with an emotional response, and the tutor is needed to keep the peace. Susan has certainly succeeded in generating discussion!

During this process, it is important that Susan herself remains calm and courteous, whether she agrees with the points of view expressed by her colleagues or not. She is suggesting possible attitudes for their discussion, which may or may not be based on her own ideas, but she must not shut out discussion by using 'well, whatever you say, I think…' terms, highly inappropriate for a philosophy student in any case. This is always important, whatever the subject: there must be a basis for rational argument, backed up by wide reading. In this case, Susan must have read the views of one or two other philosophers who disagree with Singer, so that she can introduce a conflicting point of view at an appropriate moment.

> *Key point: if your subject is controversial, give both sides of the argument calmly and courteously.*

We've concentrated on generating discussion at a seminar; you may also be asked to prepare a seminar paper or presentation. You may choose to prepare your material in the form of notes (see the use of notes in a presentation, pages 111–17), or write it out in full, depending to a certain extent on whether it is to be handed in and marked afterwards. If you write out a full script, it's essential that you don't simply read it at the group; leave spaces on the page at points where you need to pause for note-writers to catch up, highlight important points which you want to stress, and practise reading it aloud, to see whether it flows in a way that will help you as you read it and the audience as it listens. You may want to break up your paper, allowing discussion from time to time rather than just at the end; this is acceptable, but you or the tutor will need to control the discussion to make sure that you can finish what you have prepared.

It would take up too much space to give the full seminar paper that might be written in answer to the Singer question above, but we will suggest some ways in which it would be different from the discussion outline. An introduction would show how the paper is organized, including the definition (written on the board in Susan's version), and a discussion of the idea of 'non-persons' as applied to animals and people. Singer's position would be given in more detail, with a discussion of ideas of consciousness and self-consciousness. Conflicting authorities would be quoted, with the appropriate references available.

This might lead to your own views, requested in the second part of the question. These must be given objectively and with a sense of the opposing arguments — there is no easy resolution of complex issues, and you must show an awareness of this. Human responsibility in the killing of animals, and the choice of whether to eat meat or not, are issues which cause bitter argument and strong emotions, but they can be written about in a rational way.

The paper will have a conclusion, assessing the implications of the different viewpoints discussed and perhaps looking briefly at the contemporary debate. In many ways, the result will be like an essay on the subject, but in writing it, you must remember that it is primarily intended to be read aloud. Have a list of references to hand, in case you are asked to support what you say, but don't attempt to include it in your talk.

Suggest points for discussion from time to time, to encourage your colleagues to join in at the end of your paper. If people disagree with what you have said, treat their views with respect – which doesn't mean that you have to change your mind.

The main purposes of a seminar, of any kind, are to develop your abilities to present an argument clearly and coherently, in speech as well as in writing, and to help you to identify the main points in an argument and respond to them. These are likely to be important qualities during your course and in your working life.

> *Key point: support your own point of view with evidence and logical argument, be aware of conflicting opinions and treat your colleagues' views with respect.*

Guest speaker seminars

Guest speaker seminars are, from your point of view, the easiest form of seminar, but don't expect just to sit and listen. Guest speakers are invited because they are known and respected scholars who have something useful and interesting to say. It's as important to make notes on such occasions as it is at any lecture: if you don't, you will forget valuable information, and you will also lose the chance to quote it in your essay or dissertation. You might pick up an idea which hasn't yet appeared in print, and so be able to impress your reader with how up to date your sources are.

If you were the guest speaker, you would have gone to considerable trouble to prepare your paper; you might have travelled a long way to give it, and you would be hoping for a response that showed interest and appreciation. If your audience just sat at the end like a row of lemons and said nothing, you would be disappointed and probably irritated. You would want questions, and time would certainly have been allowed for them.

You, as a student attending the seminar, should be ready to ask questions. It isn't easy, especially as there may be staff, as well as other students, listening, and you don't want to look stupid. As you listen, think about what the speaker is saying, and make a quick note if there's anything that isn't clear, or which you would like to hear more about.

When the opportunity comes, review your question quickly to check that it hasn't been answered and then be prepared to ask it. Keep it short and to the point, as audiences get irritated by long, rambling questions, and smile at the speaker before you ask. When you have your answer, thank the speaker. You'll find that it will be much easier to ask a question next time; you may also be surprised to discover that other members of the audience were interested in your question and are grateful to you for asking it.

> *Key point: be prepared to ask a question of a guest speaker; he or she, and the rest of the audience, will be grateful to you.*

▶ Tutorials

Tutorials, sometimes called supervisions, take place in very small groups indeed, perhaps only you and your tutor, or perhaps you, another student and your tutor. There are unlikely to be more than three or four students in total, or else the occasion would become more of a seminar than a tutorial.

You will have handed in a piece of work, probably an essay, to be marked; you may have already received it back, with your tutor's comments. Procedures vary: sometimes the essay is actually read aloud at the tutorial; sometimes it's returned to you during the tutorial, but perhaps more commonly you will already have seen a marked version. In any case, the tutor will have more to say, in terms of what you might have included, authorities you could have cited or the general quality of your argument. Generally, the tutor will try to give you some encouragement, commenting on the good points you have made and the sensible structure you have adopted (see pages 39–46). You and your tutor now go through the essay together, discussing what you have written and how he or she has reacted. You will gain most benefit from this meeting if you prepare beforehand: read through your tutor's comments and mark any that you want to discuss further or query.

> *Key point: prepare for your tutorial by marking the comments you want to discuss in more detail.*

Remember to take notes during your tutorial. This isn't as easy as it is in a lecture, because you are holding a conversation and your instinct will be to look at your tutor and talk or listen, rather than break eye contact by making notes. Nevertheless, you will use your essay when you revise for your exams, and it will be of even more help if you have the additional information from your tutorial in front of you.

Marking styles vary. Some lecturers write copious notes on student work and almost a second essay at the end, and this is very helpful. Unfortunately, other lecturers may do little more than put ticks or underlining on the page, with no comment, and in such cases your notes at the tutorial become even more important. Don't be afraid to ask your tutor to wait a moment while you write a quick note for your own use.

Tutorials are essentially for your benefit. They give you an opportunity to ask questions in a small-group context, when the atmosphere is likely to be informal and friendly. You may be unhappy with the grade or mark you've been given. In your tutorial, you have the chance to ask why and your tutor will explain his or her reasoning. You may not understand a comment; you may disagree with what your tutor has written; you may be particularly interested in one aspect of the topic and want to ask for more information or perhaps further reading. The tutorial is your opportunity to do any of these things; to a certain extent, you set the agenda. As long as you are polite and genuinely want to know, your tutor has a responsibility to help you. If you have no questions and seem bored with the whole topic, there isn't much your tutor can do about the situation and you will be the loser.

The tutorial, especially if you are the only student present, is also an opportunity for you to ask for your tutor's assessment of how well you are coping with the course, or for you to express any academic anxieties you may have. You may want to approach a personal tutor in private rather than deal with such matters in the context of a tutorial, but there's no reason why you shouldn't ask questions in general terms about the course and the level of work required. You may also want to ask about a point that arose during a lecture by your tutor, when maybe you hesitated to ask in class. All these are possible uses for your tutorials, and your work will benefit enormously if you make the most of such opportunities.

Tutorials are a great invention, and rare in other European countries, where class sizes tend to be much bigger and the approach more formal. You are lucky to have the chance to see your tutor as a knowledgeable friend and advisor.

6   Formal Presentations

In the last chapter, we looked at talking to small groups, in seminars and tutorials; now we'll consider more formal occasions, when you will find yourself preparing to make a presentation to an audience, perhaps of only a small number of people, occasionally to a larger group. Formality is the key to the difference: a seminar, while it's obviously a serious form of communication, is likely to be quite informal, so that if it changes into a general discussion, nobody is likely to mind, or perhaps even notice. A presentation is formalized in structure and style: you will almost certainly be told how long you should speak for and when questions will be asked, and you will be expected to talk and control the situation in a professional way. In the next chapter, we'll look at the way in which you use your voice and your body language, and how you relate to another speaker if you are working in pairs; at this stage, we'll discuss how you prepare your presentation, your notes and your visual aids. At the same time, we must stress that all this preparation must be carried out with your partner, if there are two of you: your visual aids, especially, should have a similar style and layout, and you need to agree each stage of the preparation.

When might you be asked to make a formal presentation? The probable answer is 'not very often' compared with seminars and tutorials, but three opportunities may well arise:

1   You might be asked simply as part of your course to make a presentation, either by yourself or with a partner. You will (together, if appropriate) need to check aspects such as the timing and when questions and answers are expected, but you may find that after your initial talk, the session becomes more like a seminar, with general discussion guided by the tutor. The exact form of such a presentation varies from department to department and even lecturer to lecturer, but by the time you have read to the end of this chapter, you will know the appropriate questions to ask.

2   Towards the end of your course, you may have to make a presentation on the subject of your dissertation, to your lecturers and possibly to a wider audience in your department.
3   When you are called for a job interview, you may be asked to make a presentation as part of the selection procedure. This used to be rare for arts and humanities graduates, while common for students in science and technology, but it's becoming far more usual nowadays for all job applicants. It may not happen to you, but don't be surprised if it does.

The key to any successful presentation is a professional approach. It isn't easy to define professionalism, but it has to do with confidence, appearance, a high standard of material, both spoken and visual, and mutual trust – the speaker relies on the courtesy and attention of the audience, and the audience relies on the speaker to provide interesting and useful information in an efficient way. This trust is absolutely essential: if the audience trusts you as the speaker, they will forgive you if you make a few small mistakes in the way in which you present; if the audience doesn't trust you, there will be a barrier between you which it's almost impossible to break through. Later in this chapter and in the next, we will look at the main aspects of a presentation that will help you to build up this trust.

> *Key point: formal presentations require a professional approach: structure and style must be appropriate. Audience and speaker must trust each other.*

▶ Preparing your material

Choosing your topic
You will probably be given the topic you have to present, especially if the event is part of your course (see pages 201–2 for a discussion of topics for interview presentations). The golden rule is that the smaller and more precise the subject, the better the presentation is likely to be. The danger is to take too wide a topic, and then to be able to say nothing of originality or interest about it. With this in mind, look at the subject as you've been given it and see whether there is one aspect on which you could concentrate in order to say something worthwhile in a short time.

> *Key point: choose as specific a topic as possible, so that you can say something new and interesting about it.*

You might, for instance, be asked to give a short presentation to fellow first-year students to introduce them to the figure of the Greek philosopher Socrates. They will already know a little about him, especially the fact of his execution and the popular reason for it ('corrupting youth'). You could take this basic knowledge, remind people of it very briefly, and concentrate on Socrates' trial, looking at the vagueness of the charges and how far they were fabricated in revenge for the taunts of Socrates' young followers, and for some of their activities which were seen as positively treacherous. You could bring the audience's attention to the nervousness of the newly restored Athenian democracy and the potential 'threat' of Socrates' undoubted charisma. You might ask the audience why Socrates did not take his opportunities to escape before his execution, leaving this as a topic which might lead to questions at the end of your talk.

In preparing your presentation, you will of course have a great many references, to primary and secondary sources. It would not be sensible to use them in the presentation itself, but you might give them as a handout, especially if the session is to be marked (for help with handouts, see pages 119–20).

You have already the basis of a structure: a quick summary of the historical setting and Socrates' place in it; the charges at the trial, first specific (in so far as they were) and then arising from the tensions of the time, the condemnation and, if you have time, the controversy surrounding it, Socrates' failure to escape (why?) and his death. Within this framework, you will find conflicting sources: indicate the main positions they take, but avoid being sidetracked at this stage. You may need some of your background reading if you are asked questions about different scholars' attitudes to the evidence, so don't discard information which you find but don't have time for in your presentation.

Once you have the material for your talk, you need to look at how you are going to organize it in your notes, remembering that each section of your presentation requires careful attention to the audience's needs and how much you can sensibly say within the time constraints. This is particularly true at the points where you are most likely to make an impact: the beginning and the end.

The introduction

The introduction to a presentation is important: you are catching the attention of members of the audience and encouraging them to go on listening. They need reassurance. In the first couple of minutes, they will want to know who you are (unless they all know you already), what you are going to talk about, how you will structure your talk, how long you will speak for and when they can ask questions. If you don't provide answers to these questions, people will be thinking and perhaps worrying about them instead of listening. So your introduction might be in terms of:

> Good morning, everyone. As you know, I'm . . . and I'm going to talk to you for fifteen minutes about . . . after which I'll be happy to answer your questions. First of all, I'll introduce my topic, with particular attention to . . . then I'd like to spend a few minutes in describing . . . and finally, I'll highlight . . .

The audience has all the essential information and you are ready to start the main part of your presentation. There's another reason for this introduction: when people start to listen to a speaker for the first time, they take a moment or two to adjust to their own position (am I comfortable, can I see?) and to the speaker (quality of voice, clarity, perhaps accent). It's therefore a good idea to give them some 'easy' material while they make these adjustments, starting the subject itself when they are settled and ready to listen.

Once you have reached this point, the audience will be giving you a high level of concentration. It won't last, so don't waste it. Say something which will hold their interest: what is new, surprising, unusual and why they should want to hear about it. It's always useful to use 'you': 'you will know that', 'I'm sure you've found that', 'you will be surprised to hear that' and so on. This helps the audience to feel involved – and that you are really talking to them, not just to yourself.

> *Key point: reassure your audience in your introduction, and then capture their attention. Use a strong ending, to highlight your main message.*

The middle

The central part of your presentation will contain your main information, with examples and comments as appropriate. Remember that the people in front of you are listening and that human beings find listening a difficult skill. If you try to say too much in the time available, or include far more detail than they can sensibly absorb, they will shut off from you and stop paying attention. Highlight the main points you want them to remember, and then amplify these by giving examples or (short) quotations which will help to fix your message in their minds. If you feel that more detail or lots of references are needed, prepare them as a handout that people can take away with them.

The low point of the audience's concentration usually comes about two-thirds of the way through the presentation. This might be the moment to show visual aids (see pages 120–5) or give a mildly amusing or striking example. Another technique is to ask the audience a question, pause, and then answer it ('So what happened after that? . . . Well, it was . . .'). This always helps to stir up concentration and alert the listeners to the fact that they should be listening carefully.

The conclusion
As you approach the end of your presentation, let the audience know. When you say 'and finally' or the equivalent, the level of concentration will rise again, so that almost everyone will remember the last point you make. Don't waste this opportunity: say something positive, highlighting the main message of your talk and leaving it in people's minds for question time.

Above all, don't let your words peter out. Too many presentations end with 'so that's it', 'that's all I've got time for', and other such dull comments. When you've made your final strong point, smile at the audience, thank them for listening, ask for questions, stop talking, sit down and wait.

Handling questions
There will be a pause before questions, and it will feel like ten minutes although in reality it's only a few seconds. If you've done your preparation well, you can look forward to an enjoyable session; you can answer most of the questions and know how to handle the ones you can't answer. Obviously, if you haven't thought about questions beforehand, this can be the most daunting part of the whole event, but with thought and if possible some discussion with other students in your group, you should be able to predict most of the questions and decide in advance how to answer them.

If you don't know the answer, don't bluff or guess. Just say that you don't know, and you'll probably find that the audience is supportive – you can't know all the answers. If it's appropriate, ask the tutor or lecturer if he or she knows, or open the point for a short general discussion. Don't look intimidated or embarrassed; as long as you handle the situation calmly and courteously, little harm will be done. This is especially important in the interview presentation, where how you handle the question may be more critical than what you say.

> *Key point: as far as possible, prepare answers to the questions in advance, but be ready to say if you don't know an answer.*

In this chapter so far, we've looked at the structure of your presentation; now you'll need to think about making notes and deciding what visual aids you might use.

▶ Notes

In the previous chapter, while writing about seminars, we commented that you might speak from notes or a full script. In the case of a presentation, it's essential that you prepare notes, although exactly how much you choose to write out will depend on how comfortable you feel when you try out your material.

Some speakers are able to present without notes of any sort. Usually, they have a high level of confidence based on years of experience of public speaking. If you are not in this category, you will probably feel better for having some kind of prompt just in case you forget what you are going to say or the order in which you were going to say it. There is absolutely no disgrace in using notes: many experienced and excellent speakers like to carry notes, even if they rarely refer to them.

There are, however, some ways of presenting information which are not recommended. Don't be tempted to learn the whole of your material by heart as if it were a part in a play. If you do this, your 'lines' will be inflexible and any slight distraction may make you lose track of your speech; there is unlikely to be a prompter in the wings if this should happen. You may also feel that you don't want to look at the audience in case they provide a distraction; as a result, they may be left feeling that they are an irrelevance to your performance of your part.

The dangers of reading

A much more common problem is faced by people who write out every word of their presentation on A4 sheets and then inevitably read it. It takes considerable acting skill and experience to read to an audience without boring them; for most speakers, it's a highly dangerous thing to do. If you read, your eyes will be fixed to the words in front of you, so that eye contact becomes impossible – in the next chapter we'll discuss the importance of eye contact, but it's worth stressing now that if the audience is to listen to you and trust you, it's absolutely essential that you look at them.

There are other dangers in reading to an audience. We may read to ourselves at 400 or more words a minute, while in a presentation we're speaking at about 110 words a minute. When we read a script, our eyes are constantly pushing us on to a greater speed and our voice inevitably tries to follow suit; we get faster and faster, and the audience finds it increasingly difficult to hear or assimilate what we're saying. Again, you have an inflexible script, which becomes more important to you than the wellbeing of the audience. If you then take a quick glance at the people in front of you, you risk losing your place, and if you are faced with an A4 sheet full of notes, it may take you a few seconds – which will feel like minutes to you – to find the right words with which to continue.

A sheet of A4 paper is also large in comparison with a human face, and speakers are sometimes tempted to hide behind their notes; if they are very nervous and their hands shake, the papers may rustle in a very revealing way.

There is another, perhaps less obvious, hazard connected with reading from a full script. You sit down at your desk, with computer or pen, to write your notes. Your mind is at once put into writing mode, and the language which results is therefore written language – perfectly acceptable on the printed page, but slightly stiff and over-formal if spoken to an audience. When we're talking to someone, we automatically adjust our language to speaking mode, less formal, more abbreviated and probably less grammatical – but perfectly comprehensible to the listener (see page 73 where this difference of style was introduced).

We can show the difference by using the information which we've just given in two forms: a formal written style first, and then an informal spoken style.

Written language

In making a presentation, there is an additional reason for avoiding a full written text: written English is very different from spoken English. If notes are written out in full, the writer, by the very fact of writing, will naturally use a formal style which is more appropriate to a document than a presentation. The effect is unnatural and alienates the audience.

If notes consist of key words and phrases only, the speaker has to create the sentence structure as he or she is talking; inevitably, the result will be the use of spoken rather than written language. Members of the audience will feel that they are indeed being addressed by the speaker.

Spoken language

So when you're making a presentation, there's another reason for not writing everything out in full, word for word. In the English language, there's a big difference between the way we write and the way we speak. If we write everything out, then the very fact that we *are* writing locks us automatically into the written language, and then when we read it out loud, it sounds odd, like a book talking. It comes across as peculiar to the audience, unnatural and off-putting.

If we write out just the key words and phrases, we've got to *create* the sentences as we speak, and then just because we're speaking, we automatically use the *spoken* language and it sounds natural to people listening.

Analysis

Let's look at some of the differences between these two messages:

- The written form begins immediately with part of the message – 'In making a presentation...'; it uses comparatively few words, and contains no abbreviations. The spoken version starts with a meaningless word, 'so', which simply helps to launch the speaker into the talk; it contains far more words, some of which are used only to help the flow of the sentence – 'then' is a frequent example. We also see the abbreviations which we use all the time in speech, such as 'you're' and 'we've'.

- There is much more repetition in the spoken language. Statements are repeated in different words, so that the audience has a second chance to hear them. An example of this is 'writing everything out in full, word for word'. When we are reading, we can take our time over the text, and so we don't need to have information given twice in this way.

- Words can in themselves be more or less formal. 'Alienates', 'inevitably' and 'indeed' are all more common in writing than in speech (although of course we may speak them under certain circumstances); 'big', 'odd' and 'off-putting' are words which we frequently speak, but would be much less likely to write. 'Just' is a spoken variant of 'only'.

- Punctuation and emphasis are also different. In writing, we can make use of quite complex and elegant forms of punctuation, such as colons and semi-colons. In speech, it's difficult to 'say' any punctuation apart from full stops, commas and question marks. We give emphasis by the tone of voice, but this can be shown in writing only by the clumsy device of using italics. If we want to emphasize effectively in writing, we have to do it by using extra words or layout.

You will remember that the style we have adopted in writing this book is rather less formal than the example which you've just looked at, but that this was a deliberate choice in order to give the book a more friendly, immediate tone. If this were a dissertation, for example, we would certainly choose a more formal style. If we were talking to you, the style would be even less formal than it is. As we said in Chapter 3, style must be adapted to readers or listeners and objectives.

Spoken style is adapted in the same way as written style, although the differences may be less extreme. In casual conversation with friends, we use colloquialisms freely; if we share a local dialect, we may unconsciously strengthen it. When we attend a job interview, we'll try to avoid slang and we may also lose something of our local accent, especially if the interview is away from our home area. We may be unaware of these changes; they are made unconsciously because we react instinctively to differences in audience and objectives.

A presentation is a formal occasion, although the exact level of formality will vary. Even so, people tend to talk less formally than in the past, and you will happily use contractions such as 'it's' or 'won't'; it also seems more acceptable in speech to use your own experience told in the first person than it does in writing. Even in a formal context, the language is essentially spoken, rather than written, and must be so if the audience is to feel that you are talking to them rather than reading at them.

There are, then, dangers in either learning your script by heart or writing it out in full. Two forms of notes remain, both of which give a professional appearance, which is especially useful in an interview presentation, and are comparatively easy to use: visual aids and note cards.

> *Key point: don't read from a full text when you are speaking to an audience; make sure that you use 'spoken' language.*

▶ Visual aids as notes

Visual aids are primarily for the benefit of the audience, but they can also be of great use to you as a speaker. If in your introduction you present a list of the aspects you will be discussing, you are reminded of the topics and their order, just by looking at the screen. This technique could be employed at the start of the Socrates presentation discussed above. If you show a list of key points, or build it up gradually with the aid of a data projector (see pages 128–30), it will act for you as a series of prompts. Illustrations which you are projecting can be used in the same way: you may show, for example, a reproduction of an early street scene, a political cartoon or a line of music, and in each case what you see on the screen will help to remind you of what you are going to say next.

On the whole, this is a professional and efficient way of using visual aids, but there is one danger: in an unconscious attempt to see the notes more easily, you may gradually turn towards them, so that in time you are facing the screen and turning away from the audience. One way of overcoming the risk is to have an enlarged printout of the visual material on the screen placed on the table beside the projector or the computer. This must be sufficiently large to be seen from where you are standing, that is, you mustn't have to move forward to look down at the paper. If it's positioned carefully, there are now two ways of seeing the note – by glancing either at the screen or at the sheet of paper in front of you. If the image consists of a list of key points, then this can also be written on note cards, so that you can choose to look either at the screen or at the notes. Obviously if the illustration is a picture rather than words, you should be using a pointer and therefore looking at the screen in order to point accurately, making eye contact with the audience whenever possible.

In using visual aids in this way, it's very important that you are at ease with what you are showing. This means plenty of rehearsal, so that there is no sense of surprise at what is on the screen, and no temptation to peer at it in order to see what to describe next. As with any form of notes, visual aids mustn't take up too much of your attention: it's the audience that matters most.

▶ Note cards

The most common form of notes used by professional presenters is small file cards. They have great advantages over A4 paper, in that they feel firm to hold, won't rustle even if your hands shake, and are small enough to be unobtrusive from the audience's point of view. They are also too small to contain much information, and so it's unlikely that you would lose your place and be unable to find it again quickly.

Nevertheless, in preparing your file cards, it's as well to write on every other line and leave plenty of space between the main points you are making; in addition, leave a wide margin at one edge of the card for your own notes, as described later. Look back at your organization of the material, checking again the strong opening, logical progression of thought and effective ending. When you are happy with your structure, begin to make your notes, writing key words and phrases for each point, so that there are no complete sentences.

This form of note-writing helps to ensure that you will use spoken language in your presentation. As you look at each card, you'll be reminded of the point to be made but you will have to form the words into sentences as you speak. Since you are speaking to the people in front of you, you'll instinctively use a natural speech form rather than a formal written style. There is another advantage of using key words and phrases: as you rehearse, there's a slight risk that if you say exactly the same thing each time, you will start to hear yourself talking, and it can be distracting for a speaker if this happens. As you form your sentences afresh each time, the sense will be the same but the words slightly different, and the risk of listening to yourself is reduced.

The number of cards you use depends partly on how much you want to say and partly on your own experience. At first you may choose to write out most of the detail; as you gain confidence through rehearsal, you may then be ready to rewrite your notes less fully; it is perfectly acceptable to use full notes (with the provisos of avoiding sentences and leaving plenty of space) until you feel that you are ready to speak from less detailed prompts. As you finish with each card, simply move it to the back of the cards in your hand; throwing it down on the table, a common habit among inexperienced speakers, draws attention to your cards and may result in the audience counting them rather than concentrating on your message.

Content of cards

The main content of your cards will be your information, as described, but some material should always be written out, however well-rehearsed and familiar it is. If you have to introduce colleagues, put their names on your cards, as it's fatally easy to assume that you could not forget such well-known details, and equally easy to find your mind is blank at the appropriate time.

Any detail which must be accurate, especially figures, should be on the cards, as it's easily forgotten and can't be estimated or guessed. Quotations from someone else's words are also in this category, as are any references which you might need to give. You might like to highlight such information, or write it in a different colour, so that it stands out and can be seen at a glance.

Your main aim in writing notes in this way is to ensure that you give your audience accurate information in the order which seems appropriate to you, but there's a further reason for using cards.

You can write helpful messages to yourself. If you know that you tend to speak too quickly, write 'slow down' in red letters across the top of each card, so that each time you finish with a card and move it to the bottom of the pile, you'll again be faced with the message that you must remember. In a margin at the side of each card, mark where the visual aids will come – it's easy to forget a visual aid or show it too early because of nerves. If you intend to give handout material to the audience at the end of your presentation, write a message at the end of your notes, in a different colour, so that it is there to remind you at the appropriate time.

Key point: you can use your own visual aids as your notes, or prompt cards. Write out words and phrases only, not sentences.

▶ Timing the presentation

You will have been given a time limit for your presentation, and it's essential that you don't overrun. This is partly a matter of courtesy to the next speaker, but it is also a sign of professionalism; in addition it may be expedient, as you are likely to irritate the audience and so lose marks for an overlong talk. It is certainly good practice, as if you make a presentation at an interview, you will be expected to keep to time and will lose credit if you don't.

The most important way to make sure that the timing is right is to rehearse until it is. Almost certainly, you will find when you begin to rehearse that you have too much material; you have to cut it back or redraft it until you are sure that it doesn't exactly fit your time allowance but that you have a little time in hand. It seems to be a rule of presentations that things always take longer than you expect. This is partly the result of audience reaction, for which you may need to pause, and partly because of natural activity – moving into position or changing a visual aid – which is difficult to estimate in rehearsal. Most of all, it results from the use of the visual aids themselves: the time taken for the audience to see and understand an image on the screen is longer than we tend to allow for (see also page 121).

As a result of all these considerations, you will find that a presentation which is rehearsed to exactly the required 15 minutes will actually take about 18 minutes. This would be a mistake, and it's sensible to allow for the extra time you will take: if you are allowed 15 minutes, rehearse to achieve 12 minutes, so that you allow the extra 3 minutes for any unforeseen interruption or natural slowing down. Nobody is likely to worry if you finish a couple of minutes or so before time, and you will give the air of professional control that you want to achieve.

We're discussing the importance of timing in the chapter about notes because you can give yourself extra help by including timing messages on your cards. We've mentioned the 'slow down' message; you might also have a 'halfway through' card, which allows you to assess, with a quick glance at the clock or your watch, how the time is going at that point of the presentation. If you have time in hand, there is no problem; if you are running short of time, you will have to leave something out. Plan in advance what you can omit without leaving a serious gap in the argument, and put such material on a different colour card. It's extremely difficult to decide what to leave out while you are actually talking to the audience – such decisions are much better made in advance.

Just before your presentation starts, it can be useful to make a quick note on your cards of the time at which you should end. In theory, this is obvious, but if in practice the previous speaker or group overran, and you began seven minutes later than expected, it can be extraordinarily disconcerting to glance at the clock, see the time at which you expected to finish, and to remember that you have seven minutes left. It's unlikely, too, that you would remember that the difference is seven minutes unless you made a conscious effort to note it when you began.

Practise with your notes until you are confident in using them, rewriting here or there as necessary. If eventually you feel that you can manage without them, then do so, but rehearse several times without using notes, and make allowance for the fact that you will probably be nervous when you give your presentation, and you may then be very glad for the sense of security they give.

> *Key point: use your notes to help with the timing, and include any other helpful messages to yourself, using a different colour.*

▶ Handouts

Handouts can be very useful to you, whatever kind of presentation you're making. They remain with the audience as reminders of what you said and can show more detail than you could possibly project on a screen. As each person has a copy, there's no problem of visibility.

The quality of handouts must be good: they should be well-designed, clear and easy to read. Don't try to put too much information on a single handout, or the audience may be studying it rather than listening to you. Give each handout a title, so that you can refer to it during your presentation, assuming that you need to do so.

There are three possible points at which you can give your handout material to the audience, each with advantages and disadvantages.

1 Before you start, perhaps even as the audience arrives. This means that you can use the handout during your talk, but the audience may be distracted by it.
2 During your presentation, although this is sensible only with small groups, or it takes too long.

3   At the end, as the audience leaves. This makes it a useful reminder of the talk, but means that you can't refer to it at the time.

You need to make sure that there are plenty of copies of your handouts, one of each for each member of the audience, even late arrivals. Check whether you need to give in a copy of your handouts for marking purposes; if you do, keep back a clean and tidy copy when you give the others out.

> *Key point: handouts must be well-designed and not crowded. Decide when to give them out and make sure that everyone gets the appropriate copies.*

▶ Visual aids

An audience today expects to see visual aids of a high quality. We are used to seeing images which impress, on television, in advertising, in textbooks. If we have to listen for more than a few minutes without anything to look at, we tend to become dissatisfied and restless. A presenter has to be ready to hold the audience's attention not just by words but by appropriate images, indeed, it's difficult to remember a message unless it's reinforced by its visual impact.

This is the primary purpose of visual aids, to supplement the theme of the presentation and make it more memorable. Visual aids should never be used simply for their striking visual effect or their beauty, or to add variety to the presentation, although they may have all these qualities: they are there as aids to the speaker and must not overwhelm the key message.

As visual aid equipment becomes technically more complex, and the images therefore potentially more intricate or striking, there is an increasing danger that they will themselves become the centre of attention, and that a nervous speaker will try to hide behind them. If this happens, the audience has been cheated: it gave time and effort to hear this speaker, and finds that it could just as well have been sent a video, because there is no personal relationship between speaker and audience. This is the essential rapport in a presentation, and the relationship between audience and screen must always be secondary to it.

> *Key point: the most important relationship is that between speaker and audience, not between audience and screen.*

In preparing your presentation, then, you have to balance the two needs which the audience will bring to the occasion: to see and be helped by visual aids, and to build a rapport with you as the speaker. When therefore will it be appropriate for you to show a visual aid? There are innumerable answers to this question, but some of the most common are:

- to introduce yourself and your subject clearly – the 'title page' visual aid;
- to introduce the audience to the various aspects which you will talk about – this will probably be a list of words or short phrases;
- to give an overall picture of your subject before you talk about the detail, for example to show the whole work of art before concentrating on the artist's technique in a small area of the canvas;
- to remind the audience of the text you are discussing, perhaps by showing a very short extract on the screen;
- to show some process happening as reinforcement of what you are saying, for example the various stages of the correction of a text or a musical score;
- to show relationships, by a chart, family tree or flow diagram;
- to illuminate the historical or literary period you are speaking about by the reproduction of a work of art which the audience can relate to and be helped by. A map might serve a similar purpose.

All these are sensible reasons for using a visual aid, as they reinforce the message by giving additional information which the audience would not be able to gain in any other way. Nevertheless, there are serious limitations to what can be understood and remembered through a projected visual image. The audience must be able to see the illustration clearly and assimilate everything that is shown; it also needs to understand why it should take the trouble to do so. The image must therefore be as uncluttered as possible. Too much detail, or too varied a use of colour, makes this difficult; irrelevant information is particularly annoying – this can occur when a visual aid is produced from a printed original which contains material additional to the illustration. The audience often has trouble in reading such detail and cannot understand its purpose, so that the visual aid loses credibility. For the same reason, 'give-away' details such as a page or a figure number should always be removed.

There are other problems in using published material as a visual aid. The size of print is almost always much too small (an appropriate size of lettering on the screen is 30 point, and a minimum size is about 22 point; an article or an essay will probably be printed in 12 point). The organization of the page may be inappropriate for visual effect, for instance the main point may come near the bottom of the page when it should ideally be about a third of the way down the screen, where it's most easily visible.

Before deciding to use a visual aid as part of your presentation, check firstly that it's really needed to help the message. Some information is clear by itself: if the speaker says that 75 per cent of people gave a particular response to a question while a further 25 per cent took the opposite view, the audience will not need to see the figures in order to absorb the message. They will remember these proportions, which are almost certainly all that matters, but would forget the exact figures. If detailed figures are important, they can be given to the audience in a more suitable form, perhaps on a handout.

The second check is the clarity of the image. Any lettering must be large enough to be seen from the back of the room, the effect must be free of clutter or irrelevant material and the use of colour must be helpful in clarifying the image.

> *Key point: prepare visual aids in the light of the subject and the needs of the audience, and ensure that everyone can see them clearly.*

Colour in visual aids can be a great problem: it is often forgotten that a high percentage of the male population has some colour defect in their vision (this is rare among women) and a considerable number are completely colour blind, seeing the world more or less as sepia. Obviously, it's not sensible for a presenter to take account of this sad extreme, but there are particular colour combinations which can be avoided, for instance red and green, which are especially difficult to distinguish by anyone with a visual colour defect.

Some colours show up much more clearly than others: use black or dark blue for lettering, and avoid red, which is particularly difficult to see unless it is a large mass of colour, orange, which is rarely strong enough, or green, which can look washed out. There must be sufficient contrast between the foreground and the background colour: yellow or white on dark blue shows up well, but light green on dark green, or pale mauve on a deeper purple, may look acceptable on a computer screen but give insufficient contrast when projected on a large screen.

We mentioned computers. There are only two forms of visual aid in common use nowadays, the rather old-fashioned and low-tech overhead projector (ohp) and the much more up-to-date and complex data projector, operated through a PC or laptop. During your course, you may have the chance to use both of these, and we will discuss their advantages, disadvantages and ease of use in more detail. However, it's important to check what is available in your own department and take the appropriate action; ohps are widely available, but you may have to reserve a data projector a week or two before your presentation, as they are less common and much more expensive.

Before we move on to discuss visual aid equipment, it might be useful to see an example of the suggestions we've been making, remembering that whichever form of visual aids you use, it's important to organize the material and present it clearly. Using the material about Socrates from earlier in this chapter, Figure 6.1 is an example of a poor visual aid and Figure 6.2 is a better version.

As we're sure you can see, Figure 6.1 is a poor visual aid, although not as bad as some we've seen. The speaker has tried, sensibly, to give the audience a quick overview of the life and death of Socrates, before starting the presentation itself, and so has included some basic material about the philosopher's life.

The main problem is the number of words: 74 on the screen at the same time. We've enlarged the image to 20 point, which is quite small in terms of projection, and the image is crowded: this is too many words for one acetate or data projection screen. A sensible maximum is about 30 words. There are other problems with this visual aid, some of which we've listed below:

- There are, as we've said, too many words. Some are unnecessary, such as the fact that Socrates was a Greek philosopher, which the class would surely know. 'Born in' and 'died in' could also be removed, and the dates given in the usual way.
- It's rarely a good idea to show full sentences on the screen, as inevitably they involve words and punctuation which aren't needed in projected material. The final sentence in this case could either be put briefly at the start, or left out; the speaker could then say it.
- Very little punctuation is needed in a visual aid. Question marks and apostrophes should be shown as appropriate, but colons, semi-colons and so on are replaced by the spacing of the material. The image is then less cluttered.
- PowerPoint gives various options for bullet points, any of which work well. It's never a good idea to mix them, as this looks messy; two sizes of round bullets is better.

SOCRATES

- Socrates was a Greek philosopher, born in 470 BC, who:

➢ studied natural sciences before turning to philosophy;
➢ tried to make philosophy a Personal issue;
➢ pretended ignorance in order to stress people's need to ask questions.

He was:
- *Accused of creating new gods and corrupting youth;*
- *Sentenced to death, but refused to escape.*

- Socrates died in 399 BC.

SOCRATES LEFT NO WRITINGS, AND IS KNOWN TO US MAINLY THROUGH PLATO AND XENOPHON WHO KNEW HIM.

Figure 6.1 *Poor visual aid*

- Similarly, don't mix fonts. The heading, 'Socrates', is shown here in Arial Bold, which is a very heavy type face and not recommended for visual aids. The rest of the text is in Times New Roman, which is very good in printed material, but less good for projection. Use a sans serif font such as Arial.
- Italic can be useful to highlight information in a printed text, but its sudden appearance here is distracting. Don't change the style of print on a visual aid without a good reason.
- Decide whether you want to start bullet points with a capital letter or not, and then be consistent. The computer may try to force you to do so; ignore it if it isn't appropriate. Other words should have capitals only if they would normally do so, such as 'Greek'; 'personal' shouldn't have a capital.
- Blocks of capital letters are always harder to read than a normal mixture of upper and lower case. The last sentence doesn't gain by being in capitals.

Figure 6.2 is an improved version of the visual aid above. It isn't necessarily an ideal one for its purpose, as this would depend on the audience and its knowledge, but at least it avoids some of the mistakes we've listed.

You'll see that this visual aid still has too many words, although far fewer than the earlier version; the last point could easily be left out for the speaker to tell the audience. Unnecessary words have been omitted, as has almost all the punctuation. We've used Arial as the font through-out, and simplified the bullets. In the printed version, the heading is 22 point and the rest of the text is 18 point; if we hadn't been restricted by this book format, this would be different. If the visual aid is produced in landscape format, the heading can be 30 point and the rest of the text 26 point, which is a very good size for projection.

We would suggest a plain background colour, so that there's no distraction for the audience: perhaps dark blue, with the text in white or yellow. This gives a clear, professional look to the image. The heading could be the same colour, or yellow or white, whichever hadn't been used for the other words.

This visual aid could be produced by PowerPoint and then either printed onto acetate or used through the data projector. Now let's discuss both these useful forms of equipment.

The overhead projector

The ohp may be looked down on nowadays, but it has great advantages: it's easy to use, can be moved with little trouble and is unlikely to break

SOCRATES
(470–399 BC)

- Studied natural sciences before philosophy
- Tried to make philosophy a personal issue
- Stressed the importance of asking questions
- Accused of creating gods, corrupting youth
- Sentenced to death
- Refused to escape and drank hemlock
- Known to us through Plato and Xenophon

Figure 6.2 *Improved visual aid*

down; transparencies can be made cheaply, are easy to transport and can look effective. Make your transparencies by photocopying onto the right sort of acetate (as long as the original is clear enough), or by printing directly onto acetate (again, the right sort) from the computer. Hand-drawn transparencies are rarely acceptable nowadays.

Even with such a simple form of visual aid, you need to consider the comfort of the audience. An ohp switched on without an acetate in place produces an uncomfortable glare: always put your transparency in position before switching on. 'Fringe glare' or distortion can occur at the edges of the picture; correct this by using the control, or, if this is impossible, position the projector wherever it gives least distortion. If the problem is 'keystoning', when the top of the image is wider than the bottom, tilt the screen, and again move the projector around to find the best position. Avoid a bright light falling onto the screen – the ohp can stand ordinary room lighting, but sunlight directly on the screen will fade the image. The fan of an ohp is often noisy, and while you can't eliminate this, make sure that your voice can be clearly heard over it.

As with any visual aid, limit the amount of information to the most important points. If the image is crowded, the audience will find it diffi-cult to assimilate the detail that really matters. Avoid long sentences – key points are usually more effective – and check that the main message is towards the top centre of the screen. If the writing stretches towards the bottom of the transparency, it may be hidden from view by the projector itself. Remember that the lettering must be large enough for everyone to see, at least 22 point, and use a natural mixture of upper and lower case letters – text in capital letters is harder to read. Choose a sans serif font such as Arial, to keep the image as simple and uncluttered as possible.

Always use the computer spellcheck, and check the text yourself, before printing onto the acetate. Spelling errors projected onto a large screen distract the audience for as long as they are in view.

In using the ohp, there are techniques which you need to remember:

- Check that you stand clear of the audience's sight-lines: stand back, alongside the screen, so that you can see it and the audience at the same time.
- Use a pointer, and point to the screen, not on the projector; you will need to point to the important aspects of pictures on the screen, but hardly ever to words, which the audience can read for themselves.
- Always glance quickly at the screen to check that the image is straight and in focus. If it isn't, have the confidence to put it right before you speak.
- Don't switch the ohp on and off repeatedly, or the bulb may blow; it isn't necessary to switch off when you simply change the transpar-ency, but don't leave an image on the screen when you have finished discussing it.

- Allow the audience time to assimilate the whole message on the screen – don't be tempted to start talking while they are still reading. Watch them to see when they stop looking at the screen and look back at you.
- The 'progressive revelation' technique, much used by some lecturers, is not recommended. It's difficult to get it right, and audiences tend to perceive it as patronizing. Use overlays of acetate if you need to build up an image.

If you remember these points, you will find little difficulty in using the ohp effectively; the same is not necessarily true, unfortunately, of the data projector.

The data projector

The most high-tech, up-to-date visual aid equipment in common use is probably the data projector; as presenters frequently use PowerPoint to prepare their material, the term 'PowerPoint presentation' is often used to mean the whole presentation, including the use of a laptop computer and a data projector. This equipment is expensive and has to be treated with care, but if it's used sensibly, it can be very effective.

Perhaps the first, and in many ways the most important, comment about this equipment is its ability to go wrong at the critical moment. Whenever you use it, be sure that you have backup available; interestingly, the ohp has had a new lease of life as the appropriate equipment to use when you find that the data projector isn't going to work. As transparencies can be created in advance on PowerPoint and printed off onto acetate, the effect can often be just as acceptable as using anything more up to date. When you find that your laptop is not compatible with the projector, the software won't run on the equipment provided, you are networked to a different site or the whole system has crashed, you need to be able to give your presentation in just as professional a way as if everything had gone smoothly. Always have backup.

> *Key point: the more technically advanced the equipment, the more likely it is to go wrong. If you use a computer, always have backup.*

There is another decision which presenters often face. You have set up your equipment and the audience has arrived; you are ready to start, but you can't boot up your computer. Something is wrong, and you start to use the keyboard with increasing frustration in an attempt to produce the material you so carefully prepared. The audience is sympathetic – up to a point. There is a limit to the time you can keep them sitting there waiting when nothing is happening. You are, of course, also losing precious presentation time. Be ready to make the decision to stop, smile at the audience and tell them that the problem can't be overcome quickly, but that you are going to start your presentation, using your backup visual material. They will be relieved and also impressed that you had prepared for any difficulty, and therefore there is nothing for them to worry about. As long as you are clearly calm and in control, the audience will give you credit for coping with the situation.

In preparing your material, you will need to take account of many of the points made earlier about the ohp. Size of print, a sans serif font, a small amount on the screen and sensible use of colour are all handled in the same way, but there are extra considerations. You may be using a light background colour with a darker form for the print, for instance dark blue print on a pale blue background. This can look very effective, but you always need to check the image on the large screen. The colour contrast may look adequate on the monitor, but be totally inadequate when the image is projected.

Backgrounds on offer in the package you are using can also cause problems. In many ways, it is safer to use a plain colour background than to choose something more elaborate and then find that the audience is distracted. Waving palm trees or pretty patterns like wallpaper are inappropriate in a professional presentation. Even patterns which seem discreet can have an undesirable effect; if the depth of colour varies across the screen, you may inadvertently give more emphasis to some words than to others. If your chosen background includes a stripe of red at one side of the screen, this may look like underlining, and so draw attention to a point which is no more important than anything else on the screen. Again, the answer is to project your images and then look at them critically to see if there is any effect which might distract the audience from your main message.

Movement on the screen can also divert the audience. It's too easy to have points in a list appearing from the sides of the screen, rising from the bottom or moving around, when no purpose is served by this activity. If you need to show movement, then the data projector allows you to do so efficiently, but if the movement has no significance, it is better avoided. It may be more effective to show the audience the whole picture rather than build up the list one item at a time: it depends, as always, on your message. As with any other form of visual aid, the data projector must support the speaker, and not become a distraction.

In spite of these warnings, there are obvious advantages in using this equipment. You can, if you need to do so, incorporate sound, slides, a moving image or a three-dimensional illustration, and all this is under the control of the one piece of equipment. Information can be updated or corrections made at the last minute. Moving the image on is simple, whether you use a mouse, the keyboard or the remote control. You also give an impression of being up to date in your thinking, as you are clearly up to date with your visual material. However, there's a danger that you'll be so impressed by the possibilities, and so intent on making a good impression with them, that you don't allow enough time to prepare what you want to say. Don't allow the visual material to take over too much of your preparation time or attention.

In using the data projector, there are several points to remember:

- Check the lighting in the room. You may need to dim the front lights or draw a blind.
- The audience will need just as long to read the words on the screen or assimilate the details of a diagram, as they do when you're using an ohp. Stand back, check the image on the screen and don't move on until the audience is ready. You may find it easier to leave the remote control or the mouse on the table rather than in your hand; this helps you to pace your talk, and also avoids the danger of accidentally moving the image on without noticing. Use a pointer on the screen to help the audience to focus on the detail of diagrams.
- Don't try to hide behind the equipment. You should not be sitting at your laptop, you should be standing up and looking at the audience.
- Consider switching off the screen of the PC or laptop, or turning it away, before you begin. There's a temptation to look at it too often, or even to watch it as you speak, and then you're not looking at the audience.
- You may need to show an image again in answer to a question. Make sure that you know how to do this quickly and easily.
- Use a blank screen if you are moving on but have no image to show immediately – don't leave the audience looking at irrelevant material. As with any visual material, don't overwhelm the audience: your visuals are there to serve you, not the other way round.

> *Key point: know why you are using colour, choose a sans serif font and limit the amount of detail in each image.*

Try out your visual aid equipment and be familiar with it at the rehearsal stage. Think about where it will be positioned, ensuring that there is plenty of space for you. Rehearse with your visual material, so that you are at ease with it – some presenters look at the screen with evident surprise, as if they've never seen the image before. Perhaps they haven't, but this does nothing to inspire confidence in the audience. Above all, view your visuals as your servants: they must be good quality and support what you are saying. But the most important relationship is between you, the speaker, and your audience.

> *Key point: try out your equipment in advance and be familiar with it and, if possible, the room in which you will make your presentation.*

7 Delivery and Non-verbal Communication

In the last two chapters, we've looked at most of the occasions when you will find yourself talking to an audience, both during your course and when you are being interviewed for a job; we shall come back to the selection process later, in Chapter 10. This chapter underlies all the other chapters about speaking techniques, as it deals with what actually happens when you are in front of your audience. How do you relate to the people who are listening to you, and how can you put your message across most effectively?

You may come to this chapter because you want to know about seminars, you have to make a presentation or you face a job interview; there will be some differences of detail which we'll mention as the chapter progresses, but much of what you read here will apply whenever you find yourself having to talk about some aspect of your work to people who are there primarily to listen to you. You may also use the information you find here in a different way: no doubt during your time in education, you will join societies and clubs which reflect your personal interests; as you become known within the group, you may be elected to a position of authority and find that you have to introduce a guest speaker or be a speaker yourself. The techniques you will use to encourage people to listen to you on such occasions are exactly the same as those you employ during a seminar or a presentation.

▶ First appearances

The initial impact that you make on your audience is visual. You come into view and the audience makes a quick assessment – reasonably enough, as they have given up their precious time to come and listen. The way you dress will help to set the scene for the occasion: for a seminar or tutorial, which are comparatively informal, you will probably choose to dress much as usual; for a formal presentation, you will find that you stand or sit more comfortably and feel more professional if you dress a little more formally than normal – it's also true that brightly coloured clothing or ostentatious jewellery can distract from the message and suggest a too casual approach. The principal occasion on which more formal dress is essential is the interview, when you need above all to be taken seriously; we will discuss this in more detail in Chapter 10.

It's more than just a question of dress. A confident walk, a smile at the audience, obvious awareness of where to sit or stand – all these things help the audience to sense that you have a professional approach. If you shuffle in, head down, wearing a miserable expression on your face, you will have put the audience off before you say a word.

> *Key point: a presentation depends on mutual trust between speaker and audience. Make sure that the first impression you give is appropriately professional.*

Whatever the event at which you're speaking, you need to have a quick look at the room beforehand. How big is it, where will you sit or stand, where will the audience be? In a seminar, everyone is likely to be sitting round a large table, and you will talk from one end; whether you sit or stand is up to you, but you will probably feel more comfortable if you sit down, unless you are using visual aids. In a tutorial, you, any other student and your tutor are likely to be sitting as a group, perhaps round a table; your tutor may take refuge behind a desk, which will make the session a little more formal, but in many ways it's more like a conversation than a presentation.

When you are speaking more formally, in a presentation or to a society meeting, you will be standing in front of your audience, perhaps even on a platform. It's worth checking out the room as early as possible, to see if there are any major changes you need to make, such as rearranging the chairs, or even finding a more suitable venue. If you are part of a group presentation (see especially pages 148–9), you will need to discuss among yourselves exactly where you want to be: you should all be visible to the audience, but it's easier if the others sit while the speaker stands. You will also need to check where the equipment is and, of course, that you can all use it.

Just before the presentation starts, you need to make a quick assessment of any necessary last-minute adjustments. You've checked out the room and the equipment, but chairs can be moved; an earlier speaker might have moved a projector so that it's no longer in focus, you may need to set up your own equipment or boot up the computer: all these activities take time, although careful rehearsal will shorten that time considerably. Prepare or check these details before you start to speak. It's much easier to keep the audience waiting for a minute or two while you refocus the projector than to have to stop your presentation when you suddenly realize that what you are showing is out of focus and must be put right.

Don't hesitate to move anything which could present a problem. Speakers have been known to walk round a chair at regular intervals while they are speaking, apparently never thinking that it could be moved out of their way. Previous speakers may have stood at the (audience) right-hand side of the screen, but if you are left-handed, you may be more comfortable at the other side, and if that means moving a table out of the way, then move it. All these considerations can be dealt with easily and quickly before you begin to speak, and they will then cease to be either potential or actual problems. What is more, the audience will admire your foresight and confidence, in a word, your professionalism.

Whatever the occasion, your first words of greeting are addressed to the whole audience and should be spoken out clearly, accompanied by a smile and eye contact with as many people as possible. We will discuss these aspects of non-verbal communication later in the chapter (see pages 141–5), but it's worth stressing here that this initial greeting is enormously important. The audience must feel that you want to be there talking to them, whether this is true or not. When you look at them, they feel that you have come for their benefit; when you smile at them, they feel that you want to build a good relationship with them, and when you say 'Good morning, everyone', you are building on that courtesy and they know that they can hear you without difficulty. You are already forming a good relationship with your audience.

Key point: make eye contact and smile at the audience as you greet them.

▶ Using your nerves

You are very likely to be nervous at the prospect of giving either a seminar or a presentation to members of your department, and rightly so. If you are lucky, you will continue to feel nervous, even when you have become very senior in your work and used to speaking to highly prestigious audiences. The most important point to remember about nerves is that they are undoubtedly and always a good thing.

What does the audience think, when they see that the speaker is nervous? First of all, they are vastly relieved that it is someone else who is giving the presentation. 'Better him/her than me' is a common reaction. Secondly, they are rather flattered. Clearly, the occasion matters to the speaker; their reactions are important; the presenter cares about them and about the message. These are good signs to be sending out and the audience will feel them as such, always provided that your nerves don't overwhelm you.

If you are overconfident, the audience will see that very quickly, too. The message this time is that you are (too) sure of yourself, that you don't really care what the audience thinks, that you are giving the presentation solely for your own benefit. No audience likes to be treated in this way, and they will soon start to react badly to you. By the time you reach the questions, there may well be a feeling that it would be no bad thing to catch you out, and you may find that the questions are hostile and aggressive in tone. All these are obviously signs of a bad relationship between speaker and audience; you are concerned to build a good relationship which is mutually beneficial. So be glad that you are nervous – it's a strong point in your favour.

There is another reason to be pleased about your nerves. When we are nervous, we get a flow of adrenalin which makes us react more quickly. As a result, our brains work rapidly, we may remember information which we hardly realized we knew and we can think at speed about how to cope with a difficulty, should one arise.

The flow of adrenalin itself has another good effect. It adds a pleasurable tension to the occasion. The pleasure, oddly, works for both speaker and audience: it is not uncommon for student presenters to say, 'I was very scared before I started, but once I got going, to my surprise I quite enjoyed myself', and for an audience to say, 'The topic sounded rather dry, but they made it really interesting, quite exciting, in fact.' The tension flows between speaker and audience, and both, once they get used to it, find a sense of occasion, of excitement, which is itself pleasurable.

The very worst way to react when you are nervous is to worry about your nerves. The more you think about them, the worse they will get, until they begin to inhibit your thinking and you start to lose the sense of what you are saying. It is much better to accept your nerves and think of the benefits they bring: 'I'm nervous, of course, but so what? It's a good thing I am' is a sensible approach to a presentation.

Nevertheless, nerves can be a nuisance if they are allowed to be so, and you need to be aware of ways of controlling them. The first is, of course, thorough preparation of your material, so that you are totally familiar with it and are sure that it is both well-chosen and correct. Secondly, rehearsals will help you, as you will become increasingly at ease with the words and visual aids, and reasonably sure that nothing will take you by surprise. Go through your script or your notes several times, not just sitting comfortably in an armchair, but either sitting upright or standing, so that you handle your material, your voice and your body language in a way which is more appropriate to the real occasion. It's particularly helpful to rehearse at least once in the setting in which you will be giving your presentation, as the sense of having been there before removes some of the strangeness and stress. It also gives you the chance to become familiar with the equipment, the lighting of the room and so on.

You are trying to forestall problems that might arise. If you suddenly find that you can't operate the projector, of course this will increase your nerves, as will the absence of blackout when you want to use the data projector (see pages 128–30), or the awful realization that you forgot to make a visual aid which you now need. All such difficulties can be prevented if you rehearse fully in the appropriate room. There may, of course, be problems which you couldn't foresee, such as the projector bulb blowing, but even then, if you know how to get a spare and fit it, the accident won't totally destroy your confidence.

Confidence is the key word. It can exist side by side with nerves, and indeed should do so. 'I'm nervous, but I'm also confident' is a good frame of mind for a presenter, and much better than 'I'm good at this, so I don't have to worry.' (More advice about controlling nerves is given in the section about volume, page 137.)

Key point: nerves are a good thing. Be nervous, but rehearse until you are also confident.

▶ Using your voice effectively

Once the seminar or presentation has started, the speaker has to use two principal attributes: the voice and non-verbal communication (body language). Both are important if there is to be a proper rapport between speaker and audience. Those who listen must, of course, be able to hear without strain, and the essential aspects of using the voice are that it should be loud enough, clear enough and well-paced.

Volume

It's useful to ask yourself about your own voice. Do you think that it's too loud, too soft or about right? It's very unlikely that your voice is too loud; although it happens occasionally that people overmodulate for a given space (generally the effect of trying to shout rather than project the voice), it is far more common that people speak too quietly. If you feel that this is a problem, ask yourself why. Do you dislike the idea of presenting to an audience so much that you want to hide from them, physically and vocally? Think that a close friend is sitting at the back of the audience, a focus for what you want to say. Forget that other people will be there, and in rehearsal try to communicate with this one friend – you need to look at your friend and then throw your voice as far as you can.

There are other voice exercises that may help you. Say very loudly some of the explosive sounds, such as 'Bang!' 'Stop!' and 'Crash!' Shout them as loud as you can and notice how you use your mouth in doing so. Get a sense of your voice filling the space. Now try to say the words rather than shout them, moving your mouth in the same way.

You may be swallowing your voice, keeping it too far towards the back of your throat. Try humming a tune, and see how your voice is forward, in the mask of your face rather than in your throat. Humming is good, too, for breathing practice. Take a good, deep breath, filling your diaphragm rather than just your chest space. Now hum a single note for as long as you can, on the same breath. If you run out of breath in twenty seconds or less, you aren't breathing deeply enough, or controlling your breath properly (or you smoke). Put your hands on the front of your rib cage, and make sure that you can feel the air intake there; shallow breathing may be part of your problem. Practise each day, extending the length of time that you can hum on the one breath. Sometimes, for a change, start your humming and gradually get louder and then softer again. You are beginning to control your breathing, which is essential for public speaking. Usefully, you are also learning to handle your nerves, as deep, controlled breathing relaxes the body and so, automatically, the mind. Try to breathe deeply and slowly next time you feel stress, and you will immediately feel more relaxed and able to cope.

Your voice is supported by your breath, which, from a speaking point of view, is why it's so important to breathe properly. Once you are used to breathing from your diaphragm, try squeezing your diaphragm muscles gently. It's much like squeezing a tube of toothpaste at the bottom – toothpaste (or in this case more sound) comes out at the top. You can increase your volume in this way without shouting, which is unpleasant to listen to and harms the vocal chords.

None of these or similar exercises will give you a loud voice straight-away, and you will need to keep up the practice. In the meantime, try to do a bit of public speaking, even if it's only a couple of minutes to a friend, and put your breathing work into action. Remember that it will help you if you look at the audience; stand up, and make sure that your feet point towards them, so that you can't turn away and hide again. Don't look at the screen or the projector while you're talking. A certain amount of hearing is actually lip-reading and it's important for listeners to be able to see the speaker's face. Imagine that you had in the audience someone who is profoundly deaf (it could happen). That person must see your face, and is dependent upon your lip movements. Make sure that you articulate as clearly and precisely as you can; above all, don't mutter. Even if your voice is still soft, you are giving your audience as much help as possible.

Pace

The speed at which you speak is almost as important for audibility as the volume you use. Think again about your own voice. Do you think that it's too slow? This is unlikely; it's very difficult to speak too slowly to an audience, although what occasionally happens is that the speaker breaks up the flow of words with pauses in unnecessary places. Take as an example part of the introduction to a presentation:

> My presentation will last for about twenty minutes, after which I'll be happy to answer your questions.

This sentence will include two pauses, the more important of which is indicated by the comma; there is also a very slight pause after the word 'about', as the next word, twenty, is a number. Numbers are notoriously difficult to hear, and always need to be emphasized, usually by a tiny pause. The speaker whose voice tends to be too slow will introduce other pauses:

> My presentation . . . will last for about . . . twenty minutes . . . after which I'll be happy . . . to answer your questions.

The problem with this disjointed form of speech is that the audience doesn't know where it's going; they have no sense of a continuing message, and, especially when the material becomes complex, will soon lose the thread of the argument. Incidentally, that useful little pause before 'twenty' no longer helps – the pauses are too frequent to create any feeling of emphasis.

However, slow speech is a rare problem; rapid speech is all too common, and is a much more serious handicap from the audience's point of view. Words run together and can't be clearly distinguished, sentences aren't separated and so become too complicated to be absorbed and, worst of all, the audience has no breathing time in which to assimilate the information.

Pauses are an essential part of any kind of talk. Think of a good lecturer, one from whom you find it easy to take notes. Almost certainly he or she will pause to let you catch up, will stop for a second or two to let you consider a difficult point, and will use pauses for emphasis so that you know at once what is especially worth remembering. You need to incorporate these techniques into your speaking skills, whatever the occasion. However, there are moments in a formal presentation which lend themselves naturally to silence.

You are changing a visual aid, and for a few seconds your attention is removed from the audience, who are watching your actions rather than listening. You need to be silent. The visual aid is presented and the audience looks at it with interest; they aren't listening to you. If you ask them to look and listen at the same time, they will face a small crisis, and will almost certainly resolve it by looking, as the visual impact usually dominates. You have finished speaking, and your colleague is getting ready to continue the presentation; there will be a pause. You want to emphasize an important point, and you do so by pausing very slightly. You may even, if it seems wise, try a touch of humour (see pages 146–7), and the audience laughs; you wait for them to stop laughing and settle down before continuing. As you move from one aspect of your topic to another, you register the change of direction by a small pause, to allow the audience to appreciate what is happening. In the unlikely event of forgetting what you are going to say next, just pause for a few seconds while you look at your notes. This pause is particularly important: if you start to look anxious, and mutter 'erm', 'er' or suchlike, the audience immediately knows that there's a problem; if you simply pause, they will assume that it's a pause for effect and won't even realize what is happening.

A presentation is full of pauses, for one reason or another, and they are needed by the audience. If you talk non-stop, the audience will become bewildered, lose its way and eventually give up the attempt to follow what you are saying. Pauses, in addition to all their other benefits, give the audience time to think.

If you speak too quickly, you are probably not allowing sufficient silence; if you make a pause, you will also probably start to speak again a little more slowly, just because there has been an interruption.

Think about your overall rate of speech. Do you know how quickly you speak? In ordinary conversation, you probably talk at a rate of something like 160 words a minute (remember that you may well read at 400–500 words a minute – see page 18). When you are talking to an audience, you will need to slow right down to something like 100–120 words a minute, depending a little on the size of your audience. Try this, by choosing a passage of about 200 words, and reading it out loud, trying to make it last for two minutes. It will seem very strange and unnatural at first, but this is about the right speed for public speaking. Use a cassette recorder, and record yourself speaking as slowly as you can, and compare your speed with that of a very good speaker, perhaps on the radio.

Rehearse in front of one or two friends, and ask them to stop you as soon as you start to rush, or your words are indistinct. Use your notes to help, as we suggested earlier (page 117). Try to move a bit more slowly; sometimes people are pushed along by their own rapid movement, in walking into position or changing a visual aid. Your speed is, after all, closely associated with the timing of the presentation; if you have selected an appropriate amount of material for the time available, it would be a pity to spoil the effect by getting through it in half the time.

> *Key point: work on your voice until you can control the volume and pace at which you speak; remember the value of silence.*

Variety in your voice

We've stressed the importance of speaking clearly, with sufficient volume, allowing pauses and speaking slowly. When all these factors are under control, it's worth looking at the extent to which you vary your voice.

This is partly a matter of emphasis. As you make a particularly import-ant point, you need to slow down even more and increase your volume very slightly. You may also make one of the tiny pauses which we mentioned earlier, before and maybe also after this key message. In doing so, you are letting the audience know that this is something to which they should pay particular attention, without telling them so in words. When you move on to an example, or an additional piece of lesser information, speed up slightly and pull back a little on the volume. The audience will get the message, and you will be achieving variety in your voice.

Don't be afraid of a touch of drama. There is much in common between acting and public speaking, and although there are also obvious differences, you can employ some of an actor's techniques, such as holding back an important detail for a few seconds in order to draw the audience's attention to it, or allowing your tone and voice to combine in emphasizing what you are saying. Try saying an expression such as 'It's surprising that', and see what happens when you say the word 'surprising'. Your eyebrows will rise, your eyes will open wide and you will look surprised. We allow this non-verbal communication to happen in ordinary life, and it is perfectly acceptable, indeed desirable, in a presentation.

▶ Non-verbal communication (body language)

It's virtually impossible to communicate by our voices alone; this is true even if we're speaking by telephone. The recipient of our message can't see us, but we still choose the way we sit in response to the person we're talking to – upright if it's our head of department, lounging if it's a friend. Think of giving directions over the phone; you will probably indicate a left turn with your hand, or even make a circular movement when you mention a roundabout. Such body language is a normal part of our everyday life, but people are sometimes inhibited about using it when they are speaking to an audience. If you react like this, you are robbing other people of an important source of information.

There is a very important consideration about body language, which we must stress before we discuss its use in any detail: body language is closely allied to culture, and what is acceptable to one nationality may be unacceptable, even offensive, to another. If you are speaking abroad, or if your audience is of a different nationality, always check with your contact before you prepare to speak, asking whether there is anything you should particularly avoid or add to your normal response. We can't change our non-verbal communication totally, because it is so deeply ingrained in our personalities, but we can modify it a little if it seems wise to do so. In this chapter, we've assumed a Western European setting for the presentation; if this isn't right in your case, you must check all that we say and find out how appropriate it is for you.

We've already shown how we use facial expression to show emotion, in stressing the importance of smiling at the audience at the beginning of the presentation. We are registering our welcome and our willingness to talk to them. Interestingly, human beings often 'shadow' each other: if two friends are talking, they may unconsciously adopt an identical posture. When we smile at the audience, they are likely to smile back, which gives us the bonus of starting to speak to a friendly looking group. If we look dismal at the prospect of speaking to them, they will be likely to look back with a similar expression, and we have to start speaking to an apparently miserable audience.

Using your hands

Some people use their hands more than others while they are speaking; it's important not to have fidgety movements or fiddle with your hair or the pointer, but a controlled use of the hands can be effective. As we've said, we use them to indicate messages such as directions; we show size or height with our hands, or rapid movement, and all such indications emphasize the words we are speaking.

Sometimes we gesture towards the audience as a means of including them in what we're saying. 'You will all know that...' involves the audience, and we often add a gesture, such as opening our hands and moving them slightly towards those who are listening. In our culture, a closed fist always signifies aggression, while an open hand suggests friendliness and generosity.

Check, when you are rehearsing, that you have no natural hand gesture which would seem irritating or odd to an audience. Rubbing your hands together or holding your notes high in front of your chest looks strange and ill at ease; people sometimes develop very distracting habits such as unbuttoning a jacket and then buttoning it up again, repeatedly. The pointer can cause trouble: speakers extend and contract it unnecessarily, fiddle with it until it disintegrates or keep it extended and wave it around so that they look as if they are taking part in a fencing match or conducting an orchestra. Remember that the pointer is used only for illustrations, not for words, so for much of the time, you won't be using it.

Body movement

It isn't only hands which can be used to show that the audience is included; there may be moments when the speaker wants to lean slightly forward or move a pace towards them. Words such as 'You'll all agree...' or 'You've probably all met a similar problem...' suggest a forward movement towards those who are going to agree or share the problem. If, at such moments, the speaker moves back, there is an odd sense of conflict: the words suggest a good relationship – you will agree with me – but the body language suggests that the speaker actually wants to put a greater space between himself or herself and the audience, and that, in spite of the words, there is a deteriorating relationship between them.

Body language is immensely powerful. It may even override all that we are saying. 'We are happy to answer your questions', spoken brightly and positively, suggests that the speaker is really happy; spoken with a miserable look and a retreating movement, the same words create exactly the opposite impression.

Using the feet

Our feet can be a great nuisance during a presentation. Speakers sometimes shuffle as they first move into position; they shift their weight regularly from one foot to the other; they walk in a rhythmical way backwards and forwards; they rock, either to and fro or from side to side; or their feet stay together as if they were glued, and keep their owners standing to attention as if on guard duty.

All such movement, or unnatural lack of movement, is distracting and may become irritating. The best way to stand during a presentation is with your feet slightly apart and the weight evenly balanced between them. If you stand like that, you are unlikely to sway or rock to and fro, and you look reasonably at ease. If you stand to attention, you won't look at ease and there is a distinct possibility that you will start to sway.

Don't try to stand still all the time; it isn't natural, and makes you look tense and inhibited. You need a small area which is your own: any other speakers and the equipment should be outside this space, and in it you should be able to move freely. Move towards the audience when it seems right to do so; move back to the screen when you want to use the pointer. Experienced speakers allow themselves a good deal of freedom to move during a presentation, without fidgeting or creating a pattern of regular movement.

When you are sitting down in front of an audience, your feet still need to be under control. They should not tie themselves in knots, or describe circles in the air. Sit well back in your chair, in an upright position, and keep your feet on the ground. If you start to tap your foot, you are signalling impatience or irritation, and the audience will immediately wonder why. This question will interest them and hold their attention, when they should be listening to and looking at the presenter.

> *Key point: use appropriate body language; don't fidget, but don't try to keep too still.*

Eye contact

In a Western European culture, the single most important aspect of body language is eye contact. You absolutely must look at the audience. In the English language, there is a word reserved almost entirely for people who won't meet other people's eyes during a conversation: they are seen as 'shifty'. The overtones of this word are untrustworthy, not telling the truth, probably not themselves believing what they're saying, which is exactly the opposite of the trusting relationship needed between audience and speaker.

Don't try to escape eye contact. Sometimes people say that you can look along the hairlines of the listeners, or just between them, but this is bad advice. The audience will soon notice and will feel that you are avoiding them. As you move forward with your greeting at the start of your talk, deliberately try to make eye contact with as many people as possible. You may not be able to see everyone, especially if there is a big audience and the lighting has been dimmed, but at least look towards those who are sitting near the back, so that they feel that you are including them. If you do this, you will find that you have good eye contact throughout your presentation; if you avoid people's gaze at the start, you will find it increasingly difficult to make eye contact as you continue to speak.

This is just as important in a seminar as in a presentation, and is perhaps the strongest argument for using notes rather than a full script. You still need to look at your audience as much as you can; if you're working from a script, make sure you pause frequently and use the pauses to look up and round at other people before turning to your text again.

Some positions are especially difficult. If you're sitting at the head of a table, you can make eye contact with most people, except for those who are sitting immediately to your left and right. If you're standing, then check that you are in the best position for the audience to see you, but again there may be people to your right and left, whom it's easy to neglect, as they are outside your natural field of vision. Try to turn round to look at them from time to time. Don't sit or stand too much to one side of the speaking area if you can possibly avoid it, as it will encourage you to look at the people diagonally opposite you and ignore those closest to you.

Eye contact must be very brief. If you hold contact for too long, the person you are looking at will start to look embarrassed and probably laugh, and you will want to laugh in response – a distraction to you both. It should be as natural to look at the audience during a presentation as it is to look at a group of friends you are talking to and, with practice, it will be just as automatic.

Key point: maintain eye contact with as many of the audience as possible throughout your presentation.

The response of the audience

Non-verbal communication is a two-way process. You are sending all sorts of messages to your audience, and they are responding. One reason why it is so essential that you look at your audience (for more ideas about eye contact, see the section above), is that you must be able to judge their response and, if appropriate, react to it.

Tapping the foot is an obvious sign of impatience; folding the arms and frowning shows a similar irritation, or perhaps profound disagreement with what you are saying. There is little that you can do immediately, but it's worth noting that this has happened and that there are likely to be hostile questions about what you've just said. Audience body language can produce an immediate reaction: if some of the audience are leaning sideways and obviously trying and failing to see the screen, you must move out of the way. Looking at watches, putting papers in briefcases and whispering to neighbours suggest that the speaker is overrunning and had better conclude quickly. Leaning right back in the seat and looking out of the window is harder to deal with, but such actions do suggest that there is something wrong: perhaps that the audience is bored. Why is this happening? There may be nothing to be done at the time, but you can think about it for the future.

On the other hand, the problem may not be the speaker's, and this is something that it's hard to recognize while you're speaking. Audiences can react awkwardly at first because they are still recovering from the previous (awful) presentation. Someone may have to give the next talk after you, and is nervous and finding it hard to concentrate. Two people may have had an argument earlier in the day, and it is still interrupting their thoughts. Speakers often feel that the very worst thing that could happen is that someone in the audience will go to sleep. If they do, how do you know that it isn't the result of feeling unwell, having had a sleepless night or jet-lag?

Speakers inevitably tend to blame themselves, and this can affect the rest of the presentation. If there is a general reaction against what you are saying, you may face a problem, but if it's only one or two people, perhaps the others agree with you; perhaps you're right. If people look sleepy, maybe the room is too stuffy. If something goes wrong, put it right and then forget it. If you drop your notes, you may feel terrible at the time, but if you pick them up, sort them quickly and carry on, the chances are that by the end of your presentation nobody except you will remember the incident. The important message is that the speaker is in charge and can influence what happens. If you refuse to allow yourself to be distracted, and carry on to the best of your ability, the audience will probably forget what happened or if they remember, they will be sympathetic. You will lose their goodwill only if you panic, seem embarrassed or fail to carry on in a professional way.

▶ Using humour

Laughter is useful as a way of making people feel at home with one another, but when you're talking to an audience, it can be dangerous. Examine any humour which you are thinking of introducing: does it arise naturally from what you are saying? It mustn't be an 'add-on' joke; you want the audience to take you seriously, not as a comedian. Could it possibly upset or offend anyone? There is a great deal that we don't know about people just by looking at them, and we must be absolutely sure that we don't alienate anybody listening. When we're sure about these aspects, we must then be certain that if we do use humour, we can put it over well. A joke that falls absolutely flat should never have been tried; some people have a natural ability to time a line well, and others haven't. If you belong to the second category, leave humour well alone.

This advice makes one thing clear: off-the-cuff humour rarely has a place in a presentation. If you are highly experienced, totally at ease with the audience and the situation, and far too senior to have anything to lose if it doesn't work, then you might think of a witty remark on the spur of the moment and risk saying it. But a risk is still what you're taking.

> *Key point: beware of humour. If it works, it can be most effective, but if it falls flat, you will have difficulty in regaining the audience's attention and your own confidence.*

▶ Answering questions

We talked earlier about the need to identify questions and plan the answers, as an essential aspect of your preparation. How you give the answers is equally important to the total effect on the audience, and body language is involved in this, too.

There are different types of questioner. Some, sadly, will be present simply to shine at your expense; they are much less interested in what you have to say than in giving their own opinion. If you stay in academic life, you will find that such people are sometimes found at conferences. Together with this unpleasant group, we can put those who are aggressive in their questioning, trying to make you feel ill at ease. You are unlikely to meet either of these categories in an undergraduate setting, but it's not impossible.

There are two golden rules: should you find people like this in your audience, be impeccably courteous to them at all times, and use the rest of the audience – which is likely to be on your side – to help you. Think about the body language of your questioner. Hostility makes us move towards our opponent, sometimes too close for their comfort, enforcing close eye contact; we pull our eyebrows into a frown, tense up our shoulders and use our hands fiercely, perhaps jabbing with a finger. These are the responses which must be avoided. Take a deep breath, relax your shoulders, make sure that your hands are quietly by your side and smile – you are showing your opponent that you are not disturbed by what has been said, and the rest of the audience that you are calm and in control. Answer briefly and politely, and then break free of the close eye contact. Step back, look round at the rest of the audience, and ask if anyone else has a comment to make or a question to ask. You will be breaking the potentially dangerous link between you and your opponent; the situation will be diffused by your actions, and you will have created a good impression on the main part of your audience.

If you can't hear the question, ask for it to be repeated. If you still can't hear, take the responsibility on yourself or place it firmly on the room ('the acoustics of this room are difficult, aren't they?') and either answer the question that you think you are being asked, or offer to talk to the questioner personally afterwards. This latter response is useful if the question is irrelevant or unclear even after it has been repeated. If you don't know the answer, say so (see also pages 110–11), but if you can find the answer afterwards, offer to do so. Remain calm and courteous throughout, and you will retain audience goodwill.

> Key point: think in advance about possible questions and how you will answer them. Take your time, and be courteous to the audience under all circumstances.

▶ Shared presentations

You may occasionally be asked to give a presentation with one or more other people, and this is good teamwork practice. Discuss your subject, and decide how it can sensibly be divided between you. For instance, you might be studying medieval history, and two of you might be asked to talk about town life at a particular period. One person could work on the available documents, while the other looks at physical remains, perhaps with visual aids showing archaeological finds. Although a certain amount of preparation can be undertaken individually, the speakers need to come together to discuss their material, visual aids and how they will tackle questions. They will also need to rehearse together to make sure that the timing is right.

During the seminar or presentation, the speakers must support one another, by making it obvious that each is listening carefully and finding the other person's words fascinating, even though they've been repeated several times in rehearsal. If the speaker's partner looks bored, or is distracted by his or her own notes, the audience will notice and will assume that the talk isn't worth hearing. In any case, one speaker might miss out something important, perhaps through nerves, and the other speaker can supply the extra information, probably without anyone else noticing the problem. At the end of the first section, there will be a polite handover to the second participant, who will respond with a smiling 'thank you', so that the presentation continues smoothly.

It's worth saying that if you have had your partner imposed on you and you don't get on, this is irrelevant to the occasion. It happens at work and in social life, and you just have to put up with the situation. Never score points off the other person, or try to take over their work; the audience should not even suspect that there's tension between the speakers. If you find yourself in this unfortunate position, think of it as a good test of your professionalism.

> *Key point: if you are sharing a seminar or presentation, coordinate your preparation and support one another as you speak.*

▶ Improving your presentation skills

You may be inexperienced at public speaking, nervous and afraid of doing something wrong. If you have read this chapter, you will have been given a lot of good advice, but you may doubt whether you can remember it all when the moment arrives. Don't allow yourself to worry too much about this, lessening whatever confidence you have and increasing the risk of panic.

The secret is to identify any particular problem which you know is hampering your ability to speak well. Perhaps you speak too quickly. In rehearsal, concentrate on speaking more slowly, and ask a friend to stop you as soon as you start to speed up. Add helpful comments to your notes (see page 117). Then when you are at last in front of the audience, don't worry about your speed. Many good techniques in speaking to an audience are just good habits, and if you have worked hard at the problem in rehearsal, you will have started to develop the good habit of speaking more slowly. You may not yet have got your pace absolutely right, but it is better than it was, and it will be better still next time. Making successful presentations is a skill which can be learnt, although it is undoubtedly easier for some people than for others; the advice given in this book will help you, but in the end you will learn to speak to an audience by doing it and – as most people find – getting better all the time.

> *Key point: the more presentations you give, the better you will become at giving them.*

Part Four
Assessment Methods

8 Assessment, Revision and Exam Techniques

▶ Assessment

You will be looking forward to getting a good qualification at the end of your course, but in order for that to happen, your work will be assessed. Your departmental handbook will explain the details of assessment in your particular course, and we recommend that you look closely at this information as soon as you can; it's inevitably going to be different for each subject. However, the main aspects of the work that are likely to be involved are: assessed essays, project work (probably including some form of spoken communication), a long essay and/or a dissertation and an examination. Your chosen course may also give rise to very different forms of assessment, too specific to be discussed here, such as translations to and from, or an oral examination in, the language you have been studying. If you are taking a year abroad as part of your course, you may be given assessed work during that time; do keep in email contact with your tutor, and remember that deadlines will still apply. On some courses, there may even be a public aspect to your final assessment, for instance if you are presenting a fine art portfolio or giving a piano recital. If this applies to you, your tutor is the main source of guidance, but you might also be able to talk to students from a previous year, perhaps current postgraduates, and find out what advice they have to offer.

However, much of your regular work will be in the form of essays, and we've discussed these at some length in Chapter 3; have another look at our advice there to remind you of what's expected in this form of writing. Each essay that is marked is, of course, being assessed at the time, but it isn't necessarily part of your overall assessment. Needless to say, work that isn't assessed needs as much care and thought as work which is assessed, but the way in which it's marked may be slightly different: in non-assessed work, you may be given more guidance for the future, to put you on the right track so that your future assessed work is of a more appropriate standard. All marking is carried out for your benefit, not for the lecturer's, so it's a good idea to look carefully at work that's returned to you, and take note of any corrections or general comments. Remember, too, the value of face-to-face discussion with your tutor about your marks, and about standards in general. If you can't meet, then email is always available.

Most arts and humanities courses are divided into core compulsory modules and optional modules. Some of both types will be assessed simply by examination at the end, others will be part coursework and part examination, and yet other modules may be assessed totally through coursework, usually handed in before the start of examinations in other modules. It's very important that such coursework is completed as early as you can manage, so that it's 'out of the way' and doesn't interrupt revision for your exams. If you intend to write some of your coursework during vacations, you'll need to plan in advance so that you can ask advice before you leave if you need to do so; also make sure that you will have access to all the books you need. If your home address is near another university, you may be able to get permission to use the library there, but a letter from your tutor may be needed.

All assessed coursework will have a deadline. You must take notice of this, as it's difficult to get any extension unless there's a very good reason such as illness certified by a doctor; without such mitigating circumstances, you may be very heavily penalized for late work (this varies, but we've seen deductions of marks on a daily basis, so that a few days' delay could affect your final result). If you can foresee that you may be submitting work late for an acceptable reason, let your tutor know the circumstances as soon as possible. If your tutor is away, speak to the departmental secretary, as there may be a form you could complete. It's particularly important if you are a mature student with family or work responsibilities that you let your department know if some emergency makes it impossible for you to finish work on time: at least email or ring to let your tutor know what has happened. You will almost certainly find a sympathetic hearing.

All this sounds a bit severe, but you have an advantage in the mixture, very common nowadays, of examinations and assessed coursework. Some people thrive on the adrenalin produced by exams, and can call up knowledge they would never remember without that pressure; other people find the nervestrain of exams is hard to bear, and as a result they much prefer the chance to write at greater leisure. It seems only fair that both forms of assessment should be included; let's look at what each has to offer, and its disadvantages.

Continuous assessment gives you the advantage of the feedback you get from your coursework in general. Each time you are given a piece of work, you are likely to have the opportunity to ask questions about it, perhaps to discuss it with your tutor and your colleagues. You will often get helpful comments afterwards, although in the case of assessed work, you may not see it again after you've submitted it (which is a good reason for keeping a copy which could be used in revision).

Assessed work also gives you the chance to pursue your own interests in a way that wouldn't be possible in an exam. You may be taught in a small group, or even just work individually under the guidance of your supervisor, so that you can discuss the work as it develops, not just after it's completed. Within the limits of the deadline, you can organize your time as you like, to fit in with other interests and activities. Perhaps the most useful aspect of continuous assessment is that you can complete part of your work comparatively early on and avoid at least some exams!

> *Key point: continuous assessment gives you the opportunity to work in a small group or even individually, and to build on help given by your tutor, but you have to keep to deadlines.*

Nevertheless, it would be a mistake to think of exams in a totally negative way. They produce stress, but it's short-lived: you may find three hours of intense, concentrated work much more productive than a longer but less precise timetable. The work is organized for you; you know exactly when and where the test will come. The adrenalin, as we said earlier, may also help you, and it's useful in this context to think about the way you control your breathing, much as you did before a presentation. Best of all, when the exam's over, it's done with, and you can forget it, go out and enjoy yourself if you want to (unless you have another exam next day).

Continuous assessment brings its own problems. If you're not very good at time management, you may leave everything too late and then have an enormous panic which may be much more severe than the stress of an exam, not least because you are blaming yourself. You may have to juggle finishing a piece of assessed work and revising for an exam at the same time, and as a result, you may skip the essential checking, or hand in work which is less well presented than it would have been if you had had more time. You may not like your tutor, or find him or her unhelpful. (Exams are marked anonymously by at least two separate examiners; assessed work may be marked by as many as three different people, which can be reassuring.) It may be that you hesitate to try out an unorthodox idea in an assessed essay, in case your tutor hates it and you get a poor mark that affects your results. This shouldn't happen, but realistically it might, or you may be afraid that it might. Continuous assessment can induce stress for much longer than three hours, and if you are not the most highly organized of students, you may be very glad that some of your work is followed by exams.

> *Key point: exams are stressful, but some people may find it easier to answer questions in an intense, concentrated effort with a fixed time limit rather than over a longer period.*

▶ Revision

Sooner or later, but in good time, you will have to start revising for exams. As soon as you can, check all the administrative details: where each exam will take place (and, if it's a strange building, how long it will take you to get there and find the room); how long it will last; the time it starts; the number of questions on the paper, and how many need to be answered; whether the paper contains compulsory questions, and how it is set out; the style of answer which is appropriate, for instance an essay, notes and so on. It's a good idea to find out the balance of marks within each paper, as this will tell you how to allocate your time. If a question is worth at best only a few marks, it clearly isn't worth spending a lot of your precious time on it. Make sure that you know what you are allowed to take into the exam room, such as an appropriate text or document. Check all this with a friend, in case you have misunderstood something, and then make notes for yourself, so that if you suddenly wonder how many questions you will have to answer in today's paper, you have somewhere to look to find the answer. It's a good idea to do all this as early as possible, so that you can organize your revision in a strategic way, bearing in mind the sequence of the exams themselves.

> *Key point: check and make a note of all the administrative details of your exams.*

Your detailed revision plan will, of course, be dictated by your subject, but it's always worth having one, although be careful not to fall into the trap of spending so long in preparing a step-by-step breakdown of all the revision you will do that you don't have enough time left to do it. Work with a friend if you find it helpful, and together draw up a list of the topics you expect to be examined on, study past papers and listen to any clues that might be given you by your lecturers. Allocate a sensible amount of time for revising each aspect; you probably won't keep to your programme closely, but don't allow yourself to be so carried away by revising a topic that interests you that you neglect others which are less appealing.

> *Key point: start to revise in good time, and make yourself a sensible revision programme.*

Different people revise in different ways: find the style that suits you best, but don't use only this one method – a little variety makes the task more interesting. You may talk out loud to yourself or a friend; it's useful sometimes to talk through a possible answer to a question from an old exam paper with people who are studying a different subject, as their comments can be enlightening just because they aren't taking ideas for granted, and their ideas may make you see the topic in a new light. Use past exam papers, planning essays by drawing spider diagrams of the main facts, or setting yourself a test question and timing yourself as you write the answer. It may be quite a while since you wrote to time, and it's a skill that improves with practice. You may write one of your ordinary term essays within an exam-type timescale, but if you do this, tell the person marking your work what you've done, as you may then get helpful feedback, for instance that you've spent more time over your introduction than would be sensible under exam conditions. If you're very lucky, you may be in a department that sets a mock exam well before the real one; this is enormously helpful in giving you practice, but it requires considerable dedication on the part of the lecturers who have to mark the results, so you shouldn't expect it.

Record some of your notes, and listen to them while you're doing a monotonous job like washing up; some people are helped by having prompt cards placed at strategic points such as behind the taps, on the principle that you may absorb something useful almost without realizing it. Others find that they remember material they read in bed just before they go to sleep. All these ideas may help you, but don't overdo the revision: you still need both sleep and exercise, and a brisk walk in the open air helps to activate the brain.

> *Key point: find the method of revision that suits you best, but try a variety of techniques to add interest.*

Within your daily allocation, you may want to work for blocks of time as this helps you to avoid overloading yourself with information. Work for about half an hour, and then take a short break, during which you allow your mind to go back over the topic you've been studying; this will help to fix it in your brain. Make sure that you start again on time. Offer yourself 'treats': 'when I've done another half an hour, I'll have a cup of coffee', but don't then spend the following half hour drinking the coffee and chatting to a friend, unless that's in your plan, too. Try to avoid pointless interruptions which simply serve to distract you: this may involve switching off your mobile phone.

Revise at least some of the time in silence, or you will get too used to working with background noise, and in the same way write some of your work by hand if you are used to using the computer. You don't want to be distracted in the exam room by a feeling of strangeness at having a pen in your hand again. If you write slowly by hand, try to develop a quicker writing style, remembering that, whether it's fast or slow, it must be legible.

> *Key point: at times, revise in silence and write notes by hand in preparation for the exam room.*

▶ Exam techniques

Even exams vary in style, and it's a good idea to find out about each of yours as early in your course as you can. One or more may have an 'open book' style, which means that you can take an approved text into the exam room with you. We've said 'approved text', as you may be restricted to a particular type or edition, and that's also something you should check. You may have to have a 'clean' text, without written notes or colour-coding, but regulations about such details vary, and it's important to find out what your departmental rules are. The great advantage of the open book exam, of course, is that you don't have to remember your text: if it's a work of literature, you don't have to try to think of appropriate quotations, as you can look them up when you need them. The associated disadvantage is that you can spend too long in reading and so have too little time for writing. Make sure that you're as familiar with your text as possible, so that you can find your way round it without wasting time.

> *Key point: check the regulations about texts in the exam room, if this is allowed; make sure that you are already familiar with such a text.*

A variation on the open book exam involves the question being set some time before, so that you can read up as much as you want, knowing that it will be relevant in the exam itself. The biggest problem with this is usually that the same group of students wants to read the same material; this should be foreseen and multiple copies of the books needed put into a short-term loan system. Again, check this out, and contact your lecturer if you feel that people are going to miss the chance to use the books they want. Decide, too, whether you want to plan your essay beforehand (obviously a useful exercise) or spend time writing it all out for practice.

Immediately before an exam, whatever its form, you are likely to be nervous. Remember that most people feel the same, and that they, like you, cope with the ordeal. Don't, of course, take alcohol or drugs to calm your nerves, as they only slow your brain down. If you have to take prescribed medicines, check that they won't make you sleepy; if you are genuinely ill, tell your tutor or the invigilator before the exam starts; you may need a note from a doctor to confirm the problem. If you have a slight problem such as an irritating cough, tell the invigilator, who may reallocate you a seat further away from other people, and allow you a glass of water. However you feel, control your nerves as far as you can; before you enter the exam room, relax your shoulders, take a deep breath and release it slowly, exactly as you do before a presentation (see page 138).

Read the exam paper carefully, and note the questions you are thinking of answering, adding one or two 'options' in case you have second thoughts. Allocate your time between these questions, remembering that you'll need to study them and think about your approach before you start to write. Read your chosen question through at least twice, looking for the key words ('discuss', 'analyse', 'compare and contrast') and for any numbers ('choose two . . .'). Make sure that you answer the question in front of you, and not the one you would have liked the examiner to ask; however thorough your answer, if it isn't relevant, it won't get a good mark. Allow a small amount of time for checking your answers, reading them through at speed and pausing only if you want to add or change something.

> *Key point: in the exam room, read the questions and allocate your time, allowing a little for checking.*

Start with the question you like best, to give you confidence, but don't overrun your time limit. Plan your answer briefly before you start to write, not least so that if you run out of time, the examiner can see what you were trying to do. Allocate your time: as a very rough guide, if you have to write a 45-minute answer, spend about 10 minutes planning, 30 minutes writing and 5 minutes checking your work. Always answer the right number of questions: it's worth remembering the old saying that the first five marks are easy to get, but the last five are extremely difficult. Don't waste time 'padding out' your answer – the time is better spent on another question. Students sometimes have the feeling that the one who writes the longest answer wins the highest marks, but of course we can all write nonsense at great length if we feel so inclined.

> *Key point: plan what you are going to say and draft a rough structure before you begin to write. Don't spend too long on the easiest question.*

A typical arts department handbook describes what is needed for a first-class answer, and it's worth looking at this (in this case, the subject is history):

A comprehensive treatment of the topic showing a sustained, coherent, and clearly structured examination of the issues raised by the question; [the answer] demonstrates a confident command of a wide range of material, including factual information, appropriate concepts and historiography; [it] shows the ability to analyse and synthesise the different aspects of the topic, to evaluate received opinion, and to consider the subject beyond its immediate context; evidence of original and independent thought, clear writing and some stylistic flair.

The main ideas in this extract could be used for virtually any subject: coherence, confidence, the ability to analyse and synthesize, to think independently and write clearly (there is nothing about length). These qualities don't represent an unattainable dream: all students should be aiming to achieve them in their work, even if, in the nature of things, some people are more successful than others.

If you have to answer a question that you haven't prepared, don't panic. Sit for a few minutes breathing well and relaxing your shoulders, thinking about the topic and trying to remember lectures or something you have read or discussed with friends. You will probably remember enough to get you started, and you may then be able to recall information you didn't realize you knew. This is the effect of nerves, which help you to think in an alert way as long as you keep them under control. If you feel that there is more you want to say but your time allocation has run out, leave a space and come back to it later; if this brings you to the bottom of the page, write PTO so that the examiner knows there is more to come. If time is running out, you may need to answer your last question in note form; you may lose some credit for not writing it out in full, but you will gain from showing that you had the right ideas and only shortage of time held you back. Examiners, in setting the paper, will have considered how much or how little you can write in the time available, and that in itself is useful: if you find you are finishing well before the end of the allotted time, you have probably not answered at least one question fully. Use the remaining time to go back over what you suspect to be your weakest answers and consider how you can improve them. Don't assume that you have no more work to do, and walk out. If you do, you will probably remember something useful five minutes later, when there's nothing you can do about it.

> *Key point: if you're running short of time, write notes to show what you want to say.*

When each exam is over, put it out of your mind. Don't go endlessly through what you and your colleagues wrote, since you can't change it, and if you do, you will soon start to feel that they have written better answers than you have, whether this is true or not. This doesn't help your confidence. Think positively: the next paper may be much better than you expected. Promise yourself a treat at the end of your exams, so that you keep your spirits up and have something to look forward to. There is life beyond examinations!

> *Key point: don't panic! Think positively.*

▶ Vivas

Occasionally, a viva (oral test) is needed in addition to all the written exams. Unless a viva is part of the course for all students, you may think that being called to attend one is some kind of penalty, and so approach it with great trepidation or even irritation. If it happens to you, don't worry. By far the most common reason for a viva is that your exam results have fallen across a borderline between two classes of degree, and the viva is held to give you the chance to move into the higher one. It never works the other way: your grade will not be lowered because of anything that happens at the viva. You can only benefit.

> *Key point: a viva is held to help a student to gain a better result.*

Now that you know this, you can approach the viva in a less agitated frame of mind. You may be told which paper(s) you will have to discuss, and in that case, if you get enough notice, it makes sense to do some extra revision, looking especially at the aspects which you feel were weak in your previous work. You will probably be interviewed by one of your own lecturers and an external examiner, and because of the reason for the viva, they will want to help you as far as possible. If you don't make the higher grade as a result of the viva, it will be a bit of a waste of time, and so you can reasonably feel that the examiners are on your side.

> *Key point: prepare for your viva, if you have the chance, by revising the areas that were weakest in the exam.*

There's something in common between a viva and a job interview (page 197): take a deep breath before you go into the room, relax your shoulders, smile at the examiners and be thoughtful and courteous in giving your answers. Remember above all that you can only benefit from considering the implications of the questions you are asked and taking your time in answering.

> *Key point: keep calm and take time to think before you answer; you can only benefit if you use the opportunity sensibly.*

There are very occasionally other reasons for holding vivas, such as the need to help a student who suffers from a problem such as dyslexia which makes writing slow and uncongenial, or to encourage the writer of an unusually good dissertation to think about further research or publication. Both these possibilities are rare, but they are also reasons which can only be good for the student concerned. In spite of the fear they seem to inspire, vivas are not penalties, but opportunities.

Part Five
Applying for a Job

9 Preparing a Job Application and CV

Some people arrive at college or university already knowing what their future careers are likely to be, but many are unsure of the opportunities for arts and humanities graduates, apart from the obvious ones of teaching, journalism, librarianship and so on. Many graduates do, of course, enter these professions, but there is a wide range of possible careers which you may not have thought of, including human resources, the police, banking and hundreds of others. You are doing the most important work right now: training your mind and developing your range of interests and skills. A specific area of work will attract your attention, and it's worth remembering that nowadays people move from one type of job to another. Taking one promising opportunity may open the possibility of others you knew nothing about.

Nevertheless, you have to make a start, and you will probably ask for and receive advice in deciding how to choose a career from a range of sources: your tutor, professional people whom you know through vacation jobs, family links or leisure activities and, especially, your Careers Advisory Service. It's wise to make contact with careers specialists early on in your study – if you're taking a three-year course, certainly by the middle of your second year. These advisors have detailed information about possible careers, and can help you to assess yourself so that you have a clearer idea of what you are, and are not, suited to. They will also, of course, have information about vacancies, especially in local organizations, and they may suggest a vacation job which will give you valuable work experience.

> *Key point: ask advice about possible careers as early as possible; your Careers Advisory Service will be able to assess where your strengths and weaknesses lie.*

In this section, we won't attempt to discuss career choice, personality and aptitude tests, or the many ways to find a job; you will have access to plenty of help in these areas. We'll concentrate instead on the communication aspects of applying for jobs: in this chapter, completing application forms, preparing a CV and a covering letter, and writing a research proposal; in the next chapter, using communication skills successfully during job interviews.

As with so many aspects of writing and speaking, preparation is essential. It's worth looking at job adverts in appropriate journals, newspapers and on the Internet before you actually need to respond to them. Get a feeling for the way in which they are worded and the information they request – and the form in which they want it – so that you start to recognize common patterns. At your Careers Advisory Service, look at application forms to see how they are presented and the information they typically require, and think how you would respond if you wanted to apply for the job. In this way, when the appropriate time comes, you'll be ready for the long process of job hunting, and you're unlikely to be daunted by an application form.

▶ Application forms

Company forms can be unnerving at first sight: you are restricted in the amount that you can write, and yet they seem to ask far-reaching questions about you, your abilities and interests. We'll discuss a typical form in three sections, the first being a comparatively simple request for identification – your name, address, date of birth and so on. The second is likely to be a section about your academic background, examination results and work experience. Finally, and much the hardest to complete, there is the section which contains what look like the trap questions, about why you want the job and why you feel that you are suited to this type of career.

Preliminary work
It is very tempting to complete the first section of the form straightaway, as it appears to present no difficulties. Resist this temptation. Before you fill in any part of the form, photocopy it, and complete the photocopy first, putting the form itself carefully away in a folder until you are ready to handle it. Using a photocopy not only allows you to ensure that what

you want to say fits the space allocated, it also gives you the chance to have your writing checked while you can still have a second or third attempt if you need it. Furthermore, you will have a record of what you put on the form so that you can look at it again before you go to the interview.

Your photocopy should now be completed in the same way as your final version, which means that you must decide whether to write the form by hand or try to complete it on the computer. We use the word 'try' advisedly: it is extremely difficult to ensure that typed text fits exactly into the boxes provided, and the effort is probably not worthwhile. Unless you are expressly asked not to do so, complete your form by hand and in black ink – it will be photocopied by the company that receives it, and black ink gives a clearer image than any other colour (in any case, it is seen as eccentric to use any colour apart from black or blue; you want to make your mark, not be regarded as odd).

However, we did say 'unless...', and this is an important proviso: before completing any job application, on a form or in any other way, always check that you are doing what the advert or covering letter asks for; the person responsible for the first sifting of responses will almost certainly throw away any application which has not followed the style requested.

Before you start work, make sure that you note in your diary the date by which you need to have the form completed and sent off. Always allow at least three days before the deadline, as the post can let you down or a weekend can get in the way; if your form arrives late, you will not get the job, however good your results.

This is also the time to contact your referees. You will already know of two or three people who have agreed to provide references for you, and at this stage you need to decide which are the most appropriate for this particular application. Your personal tutor, course tutor or head of department will almost certainly be a regular referee, and you may also have a particular reason for choosing your second: your manager from a vacation job in the same area of work, for instance. Unless you have 'global' permission to use someone's name whenever you apply for a job, always ask before filling in the name and address, and let your referees know the type of job you have applied for, and any particular points that they may not be aware of, for example that you have worked temporarily in a similar position and therefore have experience. It's discourteous not to ask, as writing references is a considerable, and time-consuming, responsibility, and it's sensible to make sure that your referees have all the appropriate information so that they can do their best to support your application.

> Key point: take time over completing application forms; check the information in the advert, try out a photocopy first (or a spare copy if you have downloaded it), and note the date by which it has to be received. Speak to referees as soon as you can.

Facts and figures

You are now ready to complete the first part of your practice form. It seems easy, but there are dangers even at this stage. Make sure that you give your name in its official form: everyone may know you as Susie, but you are Susan on the form (unless, of course, your birth certificate refers to you as 'Susie'). It goes without saying that you must use your legal name, even if you normally use a different one (for example that of a step-parent), not least so that it's consistent with your certificates. Give your date of birth in a clear, unambiguous way: day, followed by month written as a word, and then year. You will also probably have to give your nationality and two addresses, one for term time and one for vacations.

Your term address is presumably obvious, but think about your home address. If you have two 'home' addresses, consider where you are most likely to be during the next vacation, and how quickly post could be forwarded to you if necessary. The same applies to telephone numbers (include the codes); if you have a term-time email address, then give that, too. Trying out your information on a photocopy of the form helps you to check how much you can write in the boxes: a long postal address may have to be written in small letters if the space is limited.

Other personal information may be needed, for instance your next of kin: this is not necessarily your nearest living relative, but the person who can most easily be contacted if you should have an accident or become seriously ill. You may also be asked whether you are married or not, and whether you are related to anyone in the organization. Be honest about this: if you know about the job because your favourite aunt is one of their directors, it will do you no harm to say so, and in any case it would be difficult to keep the relationship secret if you ended up working in the same building.

Other questions in this section may be about mobility – are you willing to work anywhere in the country? – and your availability for interview (if this is not mentioned, include it in your covering letter). Give yourself as much flexibility as possible in answering both these questions: if you are willing and able to live in a new area, you will increase your chances of being employed; if you are available most of the time for an interview, this is obviously helpful – but remember to exclude the time when you'll be sitting your examinations.

Education, work and leisure

The next section of the form is likely to be about your educational achievements. This is one of the places where space gives you a clue about how much to include. Start with the most recent exams, your degree for instance, as that's what is likely to be of most interest to an employer. If you passed four A levels and ten GCSEs, but the space provided precludes listing all these successes, it seems reasonable to assume that a prospective employer is more interested in your degree and A levels than in anything earlier, and you might just summarize ('10 GCSEs, including 6 A grades'). Some people have the additional problem of having moved around during their childhood, often because of a parent's job; the result is a list of schools attended which is too long for the space. If this happens, cut out the earlier schools, and mention the one at which you took your A levels.

If you still have to take your final examinations, say so, and estimate your likely class of result if you are asked to do so (having checked with your tutor first – there's no point in either under- or overestimating your results). You may also be asked about any prizes you have won, or any advanced course (postgraduate courses, for example) that you have completed; if you haven't done any of these things, just leave the section empty. There may be a section labelled 'Training', in which you can put IT skills and any courses you took while you were employed in a vacation job. As before, leave it blank if there's nothing to say. The chances are that most other applicants won't have anything to report here, either.

Above all, tell the truth. We have all heard grisly stories of people who cheated (because that's what it is) by pretending to have outstanding results which they didn't get, and whose behaviour was found out because the company asked to see the certificate (they often do), or the reference made the truth clear, or they simply met someone from their past life at the wrong moment. The reality of the situation is often discovered, and even if you get away with it, you have to live with the risk of being found out, or with the problem of trying to do a job for which you really aren't qualified. The opposite problem is much rarer, but occasionally people hide an extra qualification in case they seem to be overqualified for a particular job. They can still be dismissed for dishonest behaviour in omitting relevant information; in applications as in most things, honesty is much the best policy.

Key point: always tell the truth when applying for a job, at the same time stressing your good points.

You will almost certainly be asked about your work experience, which may relate to a year out, to part-time or vacation work or, if you are a mature student, to your previous full-time employment. The importance of all work experience is often underestimated. Include as much information as you can, and think through the experience and what you gained from it: you may be asked on the form 'Which parts of this experience were most beneficial to you, and why?', and you may have to give further details at the interview stage. It's tempting to think that spending three evenings a week working behind a bar is not much help if you are applying for a job as a journalist, but you would be wrong. You have worked as part of a small team in a restricted space and often under pressure; you have had to communicate with a range of people and keep cool if there were signs of trouble; you have had to think quickly, and look and sound friendly even if you were tired or fed up; you have had to prove yourself to be reliable. All these are highly desirable characteristics from the employer's point of view, and you may well be able to draw attention to them at the appropriate point of the form (if not, remember the interview).

If your work experience has been valuable, so too has your leisure time. Employers are interested in your outside interests because they want to know not just that you can do the job but also that you will fit into the organization, and that you will be pleasant to work with. Think through your interests carefully and, if necessary, select the most suitable. If you have too many interests, you may give the impression that you don't have much time for work; if you have only reading and watching films, you will come across as rather dull and isolated. Most jobs involve meeting and working with other people, and taking part in group activities such as team sports or amateur dramatics shows that you are used to and enjoy doing this. Ideally, you will present a mixture of interests, some involving other people, some quieter and more thoughtful.

Have you held positions of responsibility in any of your leisure activities? If so, these too may say something useful about you: if you were the treasurer of a society, people must have trusted you, and you will have gained some financial awareness; if you organized a major social event, you probably have good managerial abilities, including the very valuable ability to motivate people; if you are president of the rock climbing club, you may well be a risk-taker but you may also be ready to take responsibility for other people's safety and wellbeing.

Don't waste this valuable experience, but at the same time, take care that whatever you say fits sensibly into the space provided. Filling in an application form efficiently says something about your ability to get essential information across clearly and concisely, and that in itself is an important message.

As with exam results, also tell the truth about your hobbies. You may be asked about them at your interview, and if you clearly know very little about mountaineering in spite of claiming it as one of your interests, you will give a poor impression and could be caught out. How were you to know that one of the interview panel spends all his or her holidays in the Alps?

Two questions probably remain in this section of the form: health and additional information. The former must be handled in a straightforward, truthful way (you may have to have a medical later). There are laws about discriminating against people with disabilities, but in any case it is unwise to hide any health problems as they might cause difficulty at work later on. Many people suffer from asthma, and if you do, you would not want to be sent to work in a dusty environment.

People often undersell themselves in the 'additional information' section. Any familiarity with computers and software packages is likely to be useful – there are few jobs nowadays in which computer literacy is not an advantage. Are you familiar with any foreign languages? Even if your knowledge is limited, it is worth saying that you have a little French, Spanish or other language; it might be very useful in greeting overseas clients, even if the conversation has to switch to English. Do you have a clean driving licence? Even if you are not going to have a company car straightaway, being able to drive is always an advantage. Have you taken first aid qualifications? Any of these skills might just put you ahead of the competition, and so might win you an interview. The only piece of information which might be left, if you haven't put it earlier, is your date of birth, and so you can add it here.

> *Key point: use any work experience you have had, however unlikely or irrelevant it may appear at first glance. Your leisure activities may also provide additional, useful experience.*

What made you choose...?

The final section of the form is much the most difficult to complete. It consists essentially of two questions: why are you choosing this career, and why are you suited to this job? The wording will vary, but this is what they want to know, and much weight may be put on the way in which you respond.

So far, you have written single words, short phrases or brief sentences; at this point you will be writing perhaps a longish paragraph, half a page or even a full page, and your information is much less structured. Why have you chosen this particular career, and why do you think you are suited to it? Think back to your school days and the course you are completing, and ask yourself these questions:

- What made you apply for the course you have been taking?
- Has your perception of possible careers changed since your course started?
- Have you made choices during your course, such as which area of the subject to concentrate on?
- Which part of your course have you enjoyed most, and why?

These are only pointers, and you will want to support them by talking again to your careers counsellor, or taking an aptitude test. Don't rush this part of the form: you need to make the link between the career you want to embark on and your own particular abilities, likes and dislikes.

This will lead you naturally to consider the job itself. Think about what you know of the work for which you are applying, and again, ask questions:

- Are you likely to be part of a team, to travel, to work mainly with people?
- Is the organization large enough to offer you career choices when you are already employed, or small enough to be creating a niche for itself, to be looking for ways of establishing itself among the market leaders?

- Are you looking for the opportunity to get on-the-job training, or carry out further research, while you are working?
- Do you want to improve your IT skills?
- Is the company involved with a particular project which has appealed to you, have you tried a similar job during the vacation and found it both challenging and rewarding?

This is the kind of consideration which will help you to answer these questions. Be careful not to go 'over the top'; comments about how wonderful the company is will put off the reader because they sound false and often patronizing. Be honest about the appeal of this type of work, what you feel you would like to get out of it and what you have to offer, and write your answer simply, clearly and concisely.

> *Key point: decide why you would like – and would be good at – this particular job, and make sure that the message comes through.*

Checking and completing the form

When your photocopy of the form is complete, check it. Look up any words you are unsure of in the dictionary; ask someone else's advice about punctuation or grammar if you are unsure, and ask one or two friends to read the whole form through to see if you have left out anything important or been unclear at any point.

You are now ready to fill in the form itself. Try to do so at a desk or table, with a good light, no interruptions and plenty of time. At this stage, you don't want to make a mistake, but if you do, use Tippex as sparingly as possible, and remember to write in the correct letters when the space is dry. Fold the form as it was (or was not) folded when it reached you, and address it as indicated in the advertisement. Add your covering letter (see pages 179–82), and send off the whole application. Finally, file your last photocopied version, as you may need to look at it again later, if you are called for an interview.

▶ The curriculum vitae

Some companies favour application forms, and others prefer a curriculum vitae, that is, the story of your life. Generally, this means that you will give more or less the same information, but the format will be up to you; as a result, you will have much less guidance about the amount of detail needed, as there will be no small boxes to complete. The layout will be your choice, although there are conventions which should be followed, and the length is again a matter for you to decide. At the stage you are likely to have reached, you are almost certain to need more than one page for your CV; at the same time, you don't want it to get out of hand. Even if you are a mature student, your CV shouldn't be longer than two A4 pages. Most of all, you want to make the right impact, which means that you must draw attention to what your readers will want to know.

All this sounds daunting, but it won't be, if you decide on a simple but clear format. One of the advantages of a CV is that you can produce it on a word processor, with the help of a spellcheck and the ability to correct mistakes quickly and easily. You may even ask someone else to type up your CV for you, and if you are not good at the effective layout of information, this has much to recommend it. We're not, however, suggesting that you spend a great deal of money answering an adver- tisement offering to 'prepare a perfect CV for you'; you know more about you than anyone else does, and you should think through your CV for yourself; a little help with the typing is a different matter. One other catch is worth mentioning: if you use someone else's CV as your template, simply putting your own information where a friend's was originally, remember to check that you have changed all the details. We've heard of a case in which the original date of birth was accidentally left in place; unfortunately, the original writer was three years older, and the producer of the new CV thus had three unexplained years!

CV format

Usually, CVs, like application forms, fall into three sections. First, there is the general identifying information, such as name, date of birth, addresses for term time and vacation and so on. This is usually set out as in the example on pages 184–6. The same principles apply as with forms: use legally accepted names, write your date of birth unambiguously, think about the addresses and telephone numbers you give (see page 170). As long as all the appropriate information is given, this section is not difficult, and of course you can easily correct any mistakes or change your mind about the layout.

> *Key point: if you prepare a CV, plan its layout carefully, following modern conventions.*

As with the application form, you will need to give details of your education. You are still on the first page of your document, and you want to draw the reader's attention to the most important details. These will not be the GCSEs you obtained several years ago, but your most recent qualification (or the qualification you hope to obtain when the results are known). This must therefore come first, with the additional information needed by the reader, that is, if you are at a university, your degree result (or predicted result), and the university you attended, with dates.

You now have the opportunity to embellish this basic information. Your prospective employer will be interested to know which special subjects or options you took, and the title of your final-year project or dissertation. These details show your particular areas of interest, and perhaps also of ability; this may be crucial if you are applying to work in a highly specialized area. You may find that you take as much as a paragraph to explain all this, but it is much more important to the reader than the earlier detail, which you may summarize if you wish (see page 171).

Using appropriate headings with dates, as in the example (pages 184–6), you can now work backwards through your schooling, including your final school examination results, but probably not much detail before that. In each case, give the grades you obtained. This information may not be of great interest to the reader, but it shows your range of study; your results in English Language and Mathematics tend to be most useful in showing your basic educational level in two very important areas, and languages, for instance, are often useful even at an elementary level. However, if you are a mature student, you may wish to leave out your earlier education, especially if you have additional qualifications from a previous career which need to be included.

When you have dealt with your education, you can start a new heading, Work Experience. Again, start with the most recent, using the dates of your employment as left-hand headings and the name of your employer as a heading to the right (see example, page 185). Under this, give a short account of your responsibilities and any aspects of the job which seem particularly relevant to the post for which you are applying. Interpret this quite widely, bearing in mind the value of even the most humble of jobs (see comments above, page 172). You may write a paragraph or even two paragraphs about your most recent experience, and perhaps rather less about earlier work; list details as bullet points if it seems appropriate, but if you do this, make sure that your list has a brief introduction and is consistent in style (see section about the layout of lists in Chapter 4, pages 81–2).

> *Key point: always work backwards from the most recent experience, which is likely to be of most interest to the reader.*

If you are a mature student, you will have other decisions to make. Which do you want to put first, your academic achievements or your work experience? Only you can decide, in the light of the job you are applying for, but it's worth thinking about it and perhaps asking for a second opinion. Highlight transferable skills from your past career and academic work; if you feel that it's appropriate, explain briefly why you made the career change. Almost certainly, your maturity helped you to be a more successful student, and you might want to say that, illustrating your point with a brief example.

You've dealt with work; now your next heading is likely to be Other Relevant Experience. As with the application form, this is where you give details of languages, computer literacy, driving licence and so on. Include any sort of qualification which an employer might find useful – first aid certificates, for instance. Voluntary work, which might include valuable experience, can be given here. You are drawing attention to the qualities which make you stand out from other candidates.

This is also true of Outside Interests, which will probably be your final heading. Suggestions have been given in the section on application forms (see pages 172–3), but in a CV you have the space to say a little about these interests, especially any positions of responsibility which you have held. Don't waffle, though; this section should not become too long.

Finally, you will add the names and addresses of your referees. Give two, unless you are told otherwise in the advertisement, one being from your current educational institution and the other from your work experience, or someone who has known you well for at least a couple of years. If you are likely to apply for a number of jobs, you may want to have two or three 'other' referees, so that one person doesn't have to spend too much time writing about you; you will always need the reference from your university or college, but it is part of your tutor's job, so there should be no problem about using the same name several times. Always let your referees know anything which they might need to include, for instance extra qualifications which they mightn't know about.

Much of the information included in a CV is similar to that asked for in an application form, but there is no obvious place in the CV for the 'why do you want this career/job?' section. You will therefore need to include it in your covering letter.

However, before you start work on the letter, you need to go through the same final checking of your CV as you would with the form: is everything clear, accurate, complete, with the extra dimension – is the layout attractive and easy to follow? Have you highlighted the most important aspects?

We've produced a specimen CV for you on pages 184–6, and you might want to have another look at it before you send off your new CV.

▶ The covering letter

Every application form or CV should be sent with a covering letter. This is partly a matter of courtesy, partly in order to help the organization to which you are applying, and partly to give you a final opportunity to show that you are worth interviewing.

Every letter has a conventional format, although in practice we often abbreviate this in an informal situation, for example in writing to a friend we may not bother with our own address in detail, because the friend already knows it well. The covering letter for an application is just about the most formal letter we ever write, so every detail must be given fully and accurately.

Before you start, look again at the advertisement to check whether you have been given any guidance about the form your letter should take, for example whether it should be hand or computer written. If it is up to you, you really do have a choice: handwriting may seem more immediate and personal, and a word-processed letter more formal and professional. Either way, it must be well presented and carefully checked for possible errors either of style or writing.

The basic format for a letter includes your own address (not your name) at the top right-hand corner of the page, followed by the date, and the recipient's name and address at the left-hand side, usually positioned so that it starts a line lower than the date. An example is given later in this chapter (see pages 186–7). Give the addresses in full, including the postcode, and write the date in a modern, unambiguous way (9 May 2003 is a common and acceptable form).

At the head of the recipient's address, you will need a name. Usually, this is given in the advertisement; check that you give it in exactly the same form. If for some reason you don't have a name, for example if the advertisement simply says 'The Personnel Manager', you have two possibilities. You can address the letter in this way, in which case you are limited to the very awkward 'Dear Sir or Madam' at the beginning of the text. It's far better to ring the company and ask the person on the switchboard for the name of the personnel manager. If there is any doubt, ask to be put through to the personnel department, explain that you wish to apply for the job, and ask for the name. You are unlikely to find yourself speaking to the personnel manager, but if by any chance you do, what happens? You explain and the manager gives you the information. You are checking that the job is still available, and you can ask for a copy of the company brochure at the same time. Already, you are making a good impression as someone who pays attention to detail, and who will take time and trouble in order to get the job.

If you do this, you will be able to address your letter appropriately, which helps you as you begin to write. When you start with the name of the individual, you must finish the letter with 'Yours sincerely' (capital Y, small s), which sounds more friendly than the ending 'Yours faithfully' (capital Y, small f) which by convention has to follow an introduction with no personal name, that is, 'Dear Sir or Madam' or similar. These conventions are very strong, and you are well advised to follow them in such an important letter.

We said above that a covering letter is of help to the company. Advertising vacancies is an expensive operation, and it is always useful to know which advertisement was the most productive in terms of response. At the beginning of your letter, therefore, you need to let the recipient know how you found out about the job. First, identify the post you are applying for, if your heading hasn't already done this, so that if the company is advertising for a range of new employees, there is no confusion about the post you have in mind. Then say where you saw the advertisement, including the name of the newspaper or journal, and the date of the specific issue. If you found out about the job in some different way, for example through your Careers Office, then say so. All this is of help to the company, and it also enables you to start writing the letter in a straightforward, objective way.

You now have a small amount of space (a covering letter should not be more than one page in length) in which to draw the reader's attention to the most important features of your form or CV; tell them as briefly and effectively as you can why you want this particular job, and why you feel that you are well suited to it.

This section needs careful planning. Think in terms of four bullet points – you could write the middle of your letter in this form if you feel it is helpful – which explain your abilities and interests as clearly as possible. Look carefully at the original advertisement, and try to identify exactly what they are looking for. Do they ask for a good communicator? You might want to quote a particularly high mark which you obtained at your project presentation. Do they ask for someone to be part of a team? Remember that your project was a joint one, three of you working together, and so you have some experience of teamwork. Does the advertisement state that you would be working with customers? You met the public when you took a vacation job in a local department store. Are you likely to travel as part of the job? You took a foreign language at A level, and spent a long vacation travelling in the Far East. Dissect the advertisement and any other information you have been able to find about the company, for example through its website, to form the clearest possible picture of the kind of person they are looking for. When you have done that, match yourself to this picture as exactly as the truth will allow; choose four points which seem to be of particular importance and list them in the middle of your letter. Remember that a list needs to be introduced, and use something like 'Your advertisement asks for ability in communication and in relating to customers. These are areas in which I feel that I have particular skills and interest, as can be seen from my previous work:' and follow this with your four bullet points.

After this, you will have very little space left. Indicate when you could be available for interview, giving as much scope as possible, and when, if you were appointed, you could start work – be realistic about this, as it may be better to allow for a short holiday than to start work and then realize that you haven't had a break since you finished your exams; at the same time, don't delay the start date for too long, or the prospective employer may look for someone else who could begin more quickly. Your letter will need what is generally called a 'courtesy close' sentence such as 'I look forward to hearing from you', and then you can sign off in the appropriate form, depending on how you began the letter. Your signature must stand by itself, with no title (Mr and so on) attached to it, but you should also print your name underneath, so that it can be easily identified.

Key point: send a covering letter with all applications. It gives you an extra opportunity to sell yourself, but keep it brief. Match what you say to the requirements given in the company's information.

As before, ask a friend to check that you have written clearly and accurately; you would be well advised to photocopy both CV and letter, so that you have a good version for later use if necessary (see the following section). Use an envelope of the same colour as the paper, address it exactly according to the advertisement and send it off: use first-class post, of course, as you want to show that you are keenly interested in the job.

> *Key point: follow the conventions of letter writing, and check everything.*

▶ Online applications

Most organizations have their own websites, which often carry information about their particular requirements and their current vacancies. This is obviously a good, up-to-date way of finding out about jobs, and you may be able to order further information or a brochure online. You may find an application form which you can use via the Internet; you may also be able to email your application.

Using such facilities will speed your response, which might be an advantage, in showing something of your enterprise and computer skills. However, the responses to job advertisements may be sifted first by someone with little technical skill or interest, and an application sent online will lack the good presentation you can achieve with the printed page. There is also the danger of too swift a response: the job you get or fail to get may influence the whole of your working life, and it is worth taking time and care rather than going automatically for the most rapid form of reply.

There's another possible hazard. If the company you are applying to uses an agency to sift the applications, the agency itself may email the chosen applications through to the personnel department, thus potentially losing something of your carefully prepared layout. Take the copy of your form/CV and letter with you to the interview, so that you can produce it if appropriate – we've heard of a case in which a section of the CV, lost in transmission, was supplied by the candidate at the interview stage.

When you have sent off your email application, or posted your application form or CV, with its covering letter, you will have a long and frustrating wait to hear whether you are being called for an interview. Use this time: watch the papers for any significant news about 'your' company or that sector of industry; talk to other people doing similar work; check the company's website for any developments. This will help you to feel that you are still advancing your career, and it may be of great value if you are called for an interview.

There is one other use of this time: look for other jobs. Even though the post you have applied for seems to be exactly what you want, you may not get it. You may not even get an interview. This is very disappointing, but you will be helped by having one or two other applications in mind. Next time, you may be successful.

▶ Example CV and covering letter

As an example of all this good advice about CVs and covering letters, we've invented a graduate in history, Emily Hastings, who is applying for a job as a business administrator in a public relations company. The advert included the following information:

> The successful candidate will need good communication skills, a confident manner, creative flair and flexibility in a fast moving busy working environment.

Among the duties mentioned were: office administration, assisting with product launches and organizing business meetings and travel.

You will see how Emily has emphasized her recent academic achievements and work experience in her CV; both there and in her short covering letter, she has highlighted the factors which might make her stand out from other applicants, together with an indication of why she is attracted to this particular job. If you take this as your guideline, make sure that you think through and emphasize your achievements in a similar way. Be honest, but don't undersell your good qualities: you want the job, so make sure that your readers recognize that fact too.

The post that you are applying for may be different from Emily's, but whatever layout of CV you use, the principles are the same: keep it brief and to the point, stressing the qualities and experience which make you a suitable candidate, and presenting all the information in a clear, well-organized way.

Curriculum vitae

Emily Jane Hastings

Home address   23 Station Road, Westford, Somerset WF16 9HD
Telephone   0199 97777

I am a highly motivated graduate with administrative experience in a PR environment and a range of IT skills. An enthusiastic team player, I am adaptable, energetic and keen to learn new skills.

Key skills

- PR and marketing: my work experience enabled me to develop confidence and proficiency
- Communication: I have excellent communication skills, by telephone and in person
- Organization: personally, I am well organized and can work well on my own or in a team
- Information technology: I have a good knowledge of a range of computer packages
- Administration: my vacation work has given me valuable administrative experience

Recent education

1998–2001   University of Abimouth: 2.1 Honours degree in History

My final-year dissertation, which was awarded a first-class mark, discussed the management of the British economy at the end of the nineteenth century. This involved my carrying out independent research, some of it beyond the resources of the University, for example in libraries in London. This increased my motivation and my organizational abilities. During my second year, I attended French language classes and gained knowledge of business French.

Work experience

June–August 2000: work placement with Marketing UK

During this placement, I worked as part of a small but busy team, my duties including:

- Undertaking market research with members of the public both by telephone and in person in the town centre
- Collating and analysing the initial results of the research
- Helping to organize public events and testing sessions by selective panels
- Providing administrative backup for a team of six colleagues, including organizing meetings and travel

July–September 1999: vacation work with Southern Events Limited

During this time, I was involved with three product launches. My duties included:

- Keeping accurate data sheets to record participants' interest in each product
- Organizing meetings
- Being involved with travel arrangements
- Sourcing venues for public exhibitions
- Maintaining an extensive database

July–September 1998: voluntary work for the Wartime Museum

During my time with the museum, I was often left to work on my own at reception, answering queries from the public. My duties also included:

- Maintaining accurate records of visitor numbers
- Answering the telephone; opening and distributing the mail
- Designing a poster to publicize an event
- Contributing to the museum's newsletter

Early education

A levels in History (A), English (B) and French (A), 10 GCSEs, grades A–C, including English and Mathematics

Hobbies and interests

Reading: I enjoy modern fiction and historical and political biographies

Debating: at University, I was social secretary of the Debating Society
Cycling: I am membership secretary for my local cycling club and
have cycled at competition level
Music: I enjoy a range of music, from classical to recent releases

Additional information
- I have completed courses in Office 2000, Frontpage 2000, Excel
  and PowerPoint
- I am physically fit and a non-smoker
- I have a clean driving licence
- During my work placements, I have received training in first aid,
  and am aware of health and safety issues in the workplace
- I have a working knowledge of French, including business French,
  and some Spanish, which I should like to improve

The names and addresses of referees are available on request.

Emily Jane Hastings
Date of birth   21 May 1980   Nationality   British

Covering letter

23 Station Road
Westford
Somerset
WF16 9HD

14 July 2000

Mr Peter Jamieson
Human Resources Manager
PositiveImage Limited
33 New City Road
London WC6 9RJ

Dear Mr Jamieson

I wish to apply for the post of Business Administrator, advertised
recently within the Careers Service at Abimouth University. My
curriculum vitae is enclosed.

This position attracts me very much, as I am keen to work in a PR environment with the opportunity to broaden my work experience and be part of a team.

I feel that I have the appropriate key skills and experience, including:

- **Administration experience**, gained during a variety of vacation jobs during which I was a key member of small administrative teams
- **Excellent communication skills** both by telephone and in person with a range of clients. I was social secretary of my University Debating Society
- **Organizational abilities**, which were vital to the successful completion of my work placement, during which I worked largely on my own initiative. My undergraduate dissertation, which was given a first-class mark, required both a high degree of motivation and organizational skills
- **PR and marketing experience**, through my work with Marketing UK, which I enjoyed and became proficient in
- **Interest in and wide experience of information technology**, with experience of Office 2000, Excel, PowerPoint and so on.

As you will see from my CV, I have both relevant experience and the motivation to succeed in this post.

I am available for interview at any time and, if appointed, would be able to start work within two weeks.

I look forward to hearing from you.

Yours sincerely

[signature]

Emily Hastings

▶ Research proposals

You may have enjoyed your academic work so much, and been so successful at it, that you decide you would like to remain at university to take a postgraduate course. There are all sorts of possibilities: some courses are largely taught and examined in a way which is not very different from your first degree; others require you to carry out research and write it up as a dissertation, which will be longer than the one you wrote as an undergraduate but otherwise may not be significantly different.

Whatever type of course you are applying for, there will be forms to complete. Follow the principles we set out when we looked at job applications earlier in this chapter: fill out every form that is sent to you, carefully, accurately and in the format that is required. Make sure that you have a clear picture of all the deadlines, and that you don't undermine your case by being late in returning a form. You will find that it all takes longer than you imagined; academic referees might be abroad when you want them, and you may have to get the approval of a supervisor for the work you are proposing to start.

> *Key point: if you are applying for support for research, follow every minute instruction on the forms, and make sure you meet deadlines.*

If you are undertaking research, you will need to present a formal proposal to a funding body which, with luck, will support your work. Check them out on the Internet, in the library and in any other way you can, finding out the type of project they tend to favour; it may be worthwhile, if you can, finding out something about the members of the decision-making panel. You can't, of course, contact them, but you may be able to find out about their areas of interest and any possible bias they may have. Remember that you can get help with all this from within your own institution, your department, finance officers, or a research advisory committee.

> *Key point: do your homework thoroughly, about your proposed research topic and those who will consider it.*

Meanwhile, network as widely as you can, going to meetings and conferences, and watching out for visiting lecturers who might have an interest in line with yours. Find out about every current publication that has a bearing on the area of work you are interested in, and take every opportunity to test the viability of your own ideas.

When you come to write a proposal for your research, remember that everyone who sees it won't necessarily be as informed as you are, or as enthusiastic. You have to show that you are committed to and excited by your proposed topic, but make sure that it's as clearly written and set out as possible. First impressions count!

The panel will be primarily interested in the work you want to do, and in your academic record. Start with the research you are proposing, and back it up by showing what you have achieved so far – as usual, start with your most recent work/publication/degree, and work backwards through your academic study and your employment history. Don't go into detail unless it's directly related to your research or your qualifications for carrying out that research, and, as before, don't let the document become too long.

Key point: keep your proposal brief, clear, well-focused and enthusiastic.

You may have a long wait when you've submitted your proposal. Don't lose heart, but do keep looking for other opportunities, so that you are ready to try again if you aren't successful the first time.

10 The Successful Job Interview

A little while ago, you completed a carefully prepared, well-presented application form or CV and sent it off. You have waited anxiously for a response, and at last it has arrived: you have been asked to attend an interview. Your reaction will probably be in two stages: firstly, pleasure that your application has been so well received, and secondly, nervous tension, in case you don't live up to it in a personal interview.

Both reactions are appropriate. Employers don't want to waste their own time by interviewing unsuitable candidates, and so the very fact that you have been selected for an interview means that your prospective employer was attracted by the information you presented: your qualifications seemed appropriate, and you yourself sounded as if you might make a useful colleague. So far, so good. However, you're right to be nervous; there is always an element of the unknown about an interview, and the strength of the 'opposition' is likely to be part of that unknown quantity, as is the exact nature of the interview when it happens.

Interviews take many forms, and may include a variety of tests and exercises; you can get help with these from your Careers Advisory Service, and if you haven't already done so, make an appointment to get some practice as soon as you can. This chapter concentrates on the communication aspects of the interview, principally preparing yourself beforehand and then answering questions in a professional way. You may also have to make a presentation as part of your interview, as this is increasingly part of companies' selection procedures, and this is discussed briefly; the earlier chapters on giving a presentation are invaluable at this point.

Look carefully at the letter you have received from the company, and find out as much as you can about the form of the interview. If you are expected to stay overnight, you will be given information about accommodation; if the interview is to be on company premises, there is likely to be a map. You may be given a programme for the day or asked to bring a short presentation with you. Make a careful note of the details you've been given and think about what they reveal. It's very important that you don't miss part of the necessary preparation or make a mistake about the date, time or place.

> *Key point: before you go to an interview, find out about the organization you have applied to. Check for up-to-date information in newspapers and on the company's website.*

However, some first interviews are held on university or college premises, perhaps as part of a careers fair or 'milk round', and it's worth looking briefly at these before considering the main interview or interviews, which are likely to be held on company premises.

▶ Careers fairs and similar occasions

The so-called 'milk round' of companies on the lookout for potential employees is less popular than it used to be; you may not even be aware of it, still less take part. Careers fairs, which allow employers to exhibit their work and make contacts, are perhaps more common. They give organizations the chance to visit educational establishments, meet prospective graduates and make some preliminary moves towards attracting likely young people.

This stage is very much a two-way process. You are being given the chance to meet someone from a company you might want to work for; find out about the organization, ask questions and assess how far you are genuinely interested in the prospects on offer. You may already have been sent an application form, or you may be asked to complete one after your discussion. From the company's point of view as well as from your own, this is an introductory stage in the process.

No company wants to visit every institution of further or higher education, and so there will already have been a preliminary selection procedure; most companies look at organizations which have appropriate courses, and of which they have had good experience in the past. So if you go to an interview of this sort, you can be reasonably sure that your course has given you the right kind of background knowledge for the job. The company is also aware of this, so at this stage interviewers are more likely to be interested in different information, such as whether you show real interest in and enthusiasm for your work so far, whether you would make a friendly, cooperative colleague and whether you have business, and perhaps managerial, potential.

As a result, the person interviewing you is likely to be part of a human resources team, rather than a manager in the area in which you are interested in working. You are likely to be asked about your studies, what you enjoy and why, and about your vacation work and what you learnt from it. Remember, especially if the potential employer is a large business concern, that it has commercial interests very much at heart: practical experience, even in running a bar or meeting the public as part of your voluntary work, is of interest and probably in your favour. Teamwork is usually important, and so look for evidence that you've worked as part of a team, and that you enjoyed doing so. Sometimes students look blank because they don't feel that they've had experience of working as part of a team, when in practice they have taken part in sporting activities or amateur dramatics, when teamwork has been essential.

You may also be asked about your ability to manage your time (a successful project or dissertation might show this), your ability to make decisions (think about your vacation jobs and how you got them), your long-term ambitions (have some prepared, but don't commit yourself too strongly to what you want to be doing in ten years' time – flexibility is important!) and your ability to communicate. These are all aspects of your character and abilities which are of interest to an employer, whatever the field of work you're interested in. Of course, if there's a specific link, for example if you want to work in advertising and you've been in charge of advertising the university's summer ball, remind yourself of the preparation and planning that was involved, and the budget you had to work to, and be prepared to talk with enthusiasm about how well you did.

These are all areas of questioning which you can foresee and prepare for. In the days before your interview, think through your course, noting the parts you particularly liked or are conscious of having done well in; think about the aspects of your course which you didn't enjoy and try to analyse why; if your reasons might also apply to the work which you are applying for, you might want to think again. Remind yourself of your special interest areas or projects, and see if you can link them to the work you might be doing. Look again at the copy of your application, and decide what you might be asked about; don't undervalue your work experience, however limited – you have almost certainly had to be part of a team, been involved in decision-making and, presented your work to your peers – all these activities have given you experience which will be useful to you in whatever capacity you are to be employed.

Your next stage of preparation is to check up on your knowledge of the industry and the company itself. Talk to people who work in the same field, and to friends who have already had similar interviews. Read the appropriate section of your daily paper, look at the company's website or, if you haven't already done so, ask for a brochure. Make sure that you keep up to date with the general news, too, as it may have a bearing on your area of work; it can also sound impressive if you make a comment which shows how up to date your knowledge is and how carefully you have thought about the implications of what you have read or heard.

This first part of the selection process will probably be informal, more like a friendly chat than a formal interview, but don't allow yourself to become too relaxed. Students often find an interview on their educational premises difficult to handle just because it doesn't feel like a formal occasion; they forget to dress appropriately and tend to slouch rather than walk and sit in a businesslike way. It's also too easy to ramble in giving an answer and to say something casually which would be better left unsaid. Treat the occasion as a formal interview, and if it seems appropriate to relax a bit, do so outwardly but pay close attention to all that is said, by you or to you, throughout the conversation. Make eye contact with your interviewer and, at the end, smile and thank him or her for his or her time; this is a courtesy and also practical sense – you don't know when or how you may meet again or how influential this person may be in your future.

> Key point: at a careers fair, be courteous and formal, showing a lively interest in the organizations which are exhibiting and being positive about the experience you have to offer.

There is an overlap between the careers fair interview and the first interview proper; because of this, we'll deal more fully with appropriate body language in discussing later interviews (see pages 197–8). A modern development which may intervene is the telephone interview, a form of assessment which may become increasingly important in the future.

▶ The telephone interview

A terrible scenario was presented by Peter Kingston in *the Guardian* (*Guardian Higher*, Tuesday 2 March, 1999). It was ten o'clock in the morning and nobody was awake in the student house when the phone rang. A friend of the prospective employee answered in a befuddled way, and then shouted that 'a posh sounding geezer wants you on the phone'. The hopeful employee eventually managed to get downstairs, and immediately asked what time it was. He was told the time, and also that this was the beginning of a telephone interview for the job he'd applied for. His response to this news came in language which might be deemed inappropriate when used to a future employer. Except that by that time, the interviewer had probably become a might-have-been employer.

It's not only a dreadful scenario, it's a horribly realistic one. Employers are increasingly conducting preliminary interviews by telephone, and although in most cases the time of the call is prearranged, this cannot be guaranteed; everyone sharing the student's accommodation needs to be warned that when applications have been sent, the telephone must be answered at least politely and a message taken if necessary.

In spite of this dire warning, there are some advantages in this type of interview as long as the interviewee has advance warning. It is unlikely to be long – about 10 to 15 minutes seems to be the norm – and you can have notes prepared and available in a way which would be impossible if you could be seen. Plan what you want to ask; think of the main points of your experience and interests which you want to emphasize, and write these down in note form. While you are being interviewed, you can move reasonably freely from note to note, or add comments to your notes if it would be useful to do so.

Having prepared your notes, think about your self-preparation. Obviously, you don't have to wear a suit for a telephone interview, but you do need to think about your instinctive reactions. When you talk on the phone to a close friend, you may lean back, speak casually and even hold a different conversation with someone in the room, more or less at the same time. When you are to be interviewed, you need to have the room to yourself, if possible warning other people that you don't want interruptions. You will speak more formally if you sit in an upright, businesslike way, looking (and feeling) alert. Be ready a few minutes before the agreed time, and make sure that all your notes are within reach. Check the name of the interviewer, and make sure that your greeting is friendly and confident. Tone of voice is very important at any time, but especially so in the absence of visual contact; listen carefully to what is said and the way in which it is said, and make sure that your own response is bright and clear. Don't be tempted to talk for too long – when you have answered the question adequately, stop and wait for a follow-up. Don't interrupt, even if you are sure what the question is going to be; let the interviewer finish before responding.

Silence can present a problem in a telephone conversation, so if you need to think for a moment before answering a question, let the interviewer know. There is no disgrace in asking for a minute to think through what you want to say, and it's far better than answering off the cuff and regretting it later. You will have planned one or two questions of your own; use them if you are given the opportunity, but keep them short – the call is taking time and costing money from the interviewer's point of view. As in any interview, thank the interviewer at the end – with a smile. The person at the other end of the line can't see the smile, but can hear it in your voice. Practise a telephone interview beforehand with a friend, and notice how the voice is brightened by a smiling friendly face.

> *Key point: be prepared for a preliminary interview by telephone. Make sure that the tone of your voice is friendly and confident.*

▶ The first interview

This section discusses the first interview at which you are called to go to your prospective employer's place of work. It may be the sole interview, in which case it will take on some of the characteristics which will be discussed later in the section on second interviews, but it's quite possible that you will have two separate sessions, especially if you have applied to a large organization. If this happens, it's likely that the first will be by human resources staff and the second by a panel of senior people, possibly including the manager with whom you will be working if you are appointed.

Even before you knew that you had an interview, you were preparing for the possibility by looking out for information about 'your' industry and 'your' company. When you know that you will soon have an interview, this activity becomes even more important. You will now need to check with the Careers Service, in case they have any useful, up-to-date information; they will also, of course, help you with your general preparation for interview and may even give you a trial run.

You will be glad that you kept a copy of your application form, as it reminds you exactly what you said. Go through it, making notes of the details which are likely to produce questions, especially of the 'why do you want to work in this industry/for us' type. Clarify your answers to these questions, as they are very likely to be asked again, and now probably followed up in more detail. Think of examples from your own experience of occasions when you were part of a team, had to take a leadership role, had to explain a difficult concept to your peer group – all of these will be useful to you in answering questions. It's possible that your department or faculty will keep a book of questions asked at interview, for the benefit of future students; if so, work through it carefully, preferably with a couple of friends so that you can discuss how you would handle any difficulties.

If you are a mature student, you are likely to have more work experience than most new graduates. Be selective: plan in advance which parts of your work experience you will want to use because they are relevant to the job you've applied for, and don't be tempted to ramble. Be prepared to answer questions about your view of your new career, and why you wanted to make a change; have a vision of how you see your future which you can share with the interviewer if you get the chance. Be positive: you have much to offer.

Key point: at a first interview, you are likely to be asked about your interests, attitudes, abilities and ambitions, and similar questions designed to check whether they want you as a colleague.

There are practical considerations about arriving at the interview itself. How long will it take you to get there? Is it sensible to travel the previous day? If necessary, ring the company and ask about accommodation. If you can, go through the journey in advance, especially if you are going to drive, and so find out exactly how long it's likely to take, remembering that if you will have to travel in the rush hour, you must allow longer. It's very important that you arrive in plenty of time, that is, that you reach your destination about 15 minutes before the appointment; obviously, you will want to get to the town or city with considerably more time in hand: generally speaking, the longer the distance, the more time you must allow for hold-ups on the way.

> *Key point: before an on-site interview, check details of travel and accommodation. Arrive in plenty of time, and be well prepared.*

You must also decide on appropriate dress. This will depend to a certain extent on your area of work, but the chances are that you will need to look smart and formal – a suit and quietly coloured blouse/shirt is almost always acceptable. If you have any doubts about suitable dress, ask the advice of friends who have already been through interviews, or your tutor. Avoid anything which looks showy, such as distracting jewellery or brightly coloured socks. Check all the details – dirty shoes still act as a deterrent to prospective employers! It isn't a good idea to wear something which is completely new: it can prove to be uncomfortable, ride up in an embarrassing way or have some defect which becomes apparent at the wrong moment. Try your outfit on a few days before the interview, so that you know it will not distract you, or the interviewer, in any way.

You'll be very pleased that you've been through all this preparation when you arrive for your interview, not least because you'll feel confident that you can do your best. You'll naturally feel nervous, but as with a presentation (see pages 135–6), this is a good thing; it would be a serious disadvantage to be overconfident or casual, especially if your interviewers were aware of this, as is likely, given their training and experience. They won't worry in the slightest if you appear to be nervous, as long as you don't let the nerves overwhelm you.

When you reach your destination, explain to the person on the reception desk that you have come for interview, and give the interviewer's name and the time at which you are expected. If you have to sit and wait, look at a company brochure or magazine, as it might give you a useful piece of information. You may find that other candidates are waiting at the same time; greet them in a friendly way, but don't start asking questions. If you do, they may sound better qualified than you, and this would undermine your confidence; don't try to put them down in any way, not least since you might have to work with them in the future.

As you wait, try some breathing exercises, as you did before you last made a presentation. Take a deep breath, hold it and then let it out slowly, in a controlled way. Check that your shoulders aren't hunched up by the tension, and then breathe in the same way again. This will help you to relax and feel more confident.

When you are asked to go in for your interview, walk briskly with your head up, smile at the interviewers (there may be just one, but it's more likely that you will have a panel) and wait. One of them will probably greet you (respond with a smile), introduce himself or herself and offer to shake hands. Do so firmly; a limp handshake can be off-putting. Follow the pattern indicated: you may need to shake hands with each member of the panel or just with the person chairing the session; sit down only when invited (sit back in your chair so that you appear upright and alert; don't fidget). Almost certainly the first one or two questions will be intended to help you relax, so they will be easy to answer: 'Did you find us easily?', 'Did you have a good journey?', 'Have you been to this city/area before?' Give your answers clearly and briefly; they certainly don't want a blow by blow account of the problems you had finding the right bus.

All this is preamble, but an important part of the interview. There is courtesy on the part of the interviewers; indeed, if they didn't introduce themselves and give you a chance to settle down, you would start to have reservations about them. After all, you want to know whether they would make good colleagues for you, as well as the other way round. In these first few minutes, a great deal of communication is taking place, although only a small part of it is in words. They are assessing you: do you appear confident (but not too much so); do you respond swiftly and easily to them; is your general appearance appropriate; do you make eye contact immediately when someone speaks to you? Don't under-estimate the impact of these things; what they may really be checking is how you would appear to one of their customers. Would your manner create an immediate good impression, even if you were under pressure at the time, as you are at present?

Key point: remember the importance of first impressions, yours as well as theirs. How would you appear to a customer; do they seem to you to be desirable colleagues?

After the first few minutes, the questions will be more incisive and perhaps challenging. Think ahead as far as you can: an apparently simple question may be followed up by a more searching one. 'Are you good at communicating with a wide range of people?' 'Yes' (of course). 'So, tell me about some of the difficulties you met when you were working at reception during your vacation job'/ 'How did you deal with trouble-makers when you worked in the bar?' (You need to have thought about this, and perhaps identified a problem you handled particularly well.)

Some questions have a built-in trap which you might not see until it's too late. 'Do you see yourself primarily as a good team player or as a leader?' is typical of this type: say that you're a good team player and you might be saying that you lack leadership qualities; say that you're a natural leader and you sound arrogant. Refuse to pigeon-hole yourself. Say that it depends on the circumstances, that you've always enjoyed being part of a team but you did take particular responsibility for . . . and you feel that when you've had more work experience, you'd enjoy the challenge . . . . Let them see that you want to keep your options open – and that you can recognize a catch question when you see one. As you answer, make eye contact with the questioner, and from time to time with the other interviewers too.

If you don't understand a question, ask for it to be repeated. If you don't know the answer, say so. There is no disgrace in asking for clarification, or being honest enough to admit ignorance, but trying to bluff or pretending to know when you don't is always dangerous. If you respond like this, you may be seen as the sort of person who in the future would take chances which involve the wellbeing of other people or large amounts of company money.

On the whole, it's better to give a short answer, as long as it isn't clearly inadequate, than to talk too much. The questioner can always ask for more information or you could offer it: 'As you can see, I'm very enthusiastic about this, and I can go into more detail if you'd like me to.' This allows the interviewer to take the initiative, but gives you the chance to show that you are confident in your own knowledge.

You will probably be asked about your hopes for the future, your leisure activities (think in advance how they relate to work experience: teamwork, making decisions, deep concentration, ability to work independently), any language ability or other skill you've mentioned on your application form; perhaps (a tricky question) how you would expect the company to develop your skills in the future.

If you are a mature student, you might be asked about your willingness to work for a 'starting graduate' salary; it's worth thinking in advance how little you can realistically accept, but if you need experience in a new career, you'll want to accept whatever you think is possible, if you like the sound of the job.

You will also be asked if there is anything you'd like to ask them. Prepare two or three questions: further training is always a good subject to discuss, or opportunities to find out about different areas of the company's work or to use a particular skill. Never ask about money! If you find that all your questions have already been answered, say so, and thank your interviewers.

You are still being interviewed until the door has closed behind you. Don't look relieved that it's over, heave a sigh, slump in your chair or rush out of the room. You might be stopped at the last minute with an extra question, and you are certainly being watched. Having thanked your interviewers with a smile, you walk steadily and confidently out, close the door behind you and then relax.

▶ The second interview

It would be lovely, in that first feeling of relief that your interview is over, to think that you would now be offered a job. This may happen, but quite possibly the whole ordeal will be repeated in a further – and usually more testing – interview at the employer's premises. At least you have the comfort of knowing that you passed the first test and the company is sufficiently impressed to want see you again.

Assuming that you still want the job, you need to prepare in the same way for the second interview: find out all you can about your pro- spective employer, read good newspapers and check the Internet, and discuss interview techniques with colleagues and your careers advisors. There is more: this second interview will almost certainly be more challenging, and you need to prepare for what are likely to be the hardest questions.

You will now be facing people who have expertise in your chosen area of work; they may include your future line manager. The organiza- tion liked the sound of you as a person in your first interview, and now they want to make sure that you are among the brightest and most enthusiastic of all the young people available. Go back yet again to your course, analyse especially any choices you had to make about special subjects; think of possible commercial, political and social implications of your final year's work and especially your dissertation. Think about your work experience or voluntary work, and how it might relate to that carried out by the company.

As you look back at the experience you have had, both during your course and in your time at work, prepare specific examples which you might be able to use in answering questions. When did you have to make a quick decision under stress? How did you handle a tricky situation, or a difficult customer? If you have a few such incidents ready, you will feel more confident that you can produce appropriate evidence to show what a good employee you will be.

This is likely to be a longer interview and you may be required to prepare material in advance, especially a presentation. You've probably made presentations as part of your course, so it's a good idea to look at any handouts you were given, and to reread Chapters 6 and 7 of this book.

You may, although at this stage it's unlikely, be given a topic to research and present. This has the advantage of giving you a starting point; you will almost certainly have to narrow the topic down to be able to deal adequately with your material in the time allotted (probably about 10 minutes). Don't panic if the subject is one about which you don't know much. Others will be in the same position, and you know from experience how little you can actually say in such a limited time. Research your limited area as thoroughly as time permits, and ask advice from your tutor or appropriate lecturer.

It's much more likely, however, that you will either be told to prepare a short presentation about some topic connected with the job, or that you will be given a totally free hand: 'present on any subject you like'. Let's look at the former situation first.

You probably have a little knowledge about what might be involved in the work you're applying for, so you won't be starting totally from scratch. You may be able to find useful information from the company's own website or your careers advisors. One of your lecturers might be able to help: for instance, if the topic is to do with marketing, a lecturer in the subject would not only be able to give you some general advice, but would also be likely to suggest useful reading. Try to make what you say personal, without trying to sound as if you're an authority when obviously you aren't, yet. Include a good idea of your own, or a comment on some recent development that has intrigued you, but be willing to add that you'd like to find out more when the opportunity arises. You know how little you can say in 10 minutes: concentrate on saying a small amount as effectively as you can.

If you are given a completely free choice, in some ways you have a much bigger problem. Your first decision is whether to talk about work at all. Your second is to find a topic which is small enough to be handled reasonably in a very short time. Your third is rather different: choosing something which will make you stand out. You may need to look carefully at your outside interests. Is there anything which is unusual? Have you travelled in a remote, perhaps dangerous, part of the world?

(Remember that nowadays students often travel widely, and you don't want to give the third presentation of the day on adventures in Thailand.) In talking about this subject with newly employed graduates, we heard that a memorable presentation had been given on the technicalities of bell-ringing (it had been followed quickly by the offer of a job). However, you can't at this stage develop an exotic hobby in time for the interview, so you may need to look again at work experience, or, if absolutely necessary, at your course. Your choice shouldn't be trivial, but it should be something in which you are genuinely interested.

When you have chosen your topic, you need to prepare it in line with advice given earlier in this book. A useful comment was made by a regular interviewer in a large organization. He pointed out that one of the prime characteristics of prospective employees which interested the company was self-organization. Can you prioritize? How is your time management? Can you work well under time pressure? One very good way in which he felt that he could assess the answer to these important questions was through the presentation. Did the candidate keep to the time given? Had the preparation itself been well organized? A common problem, he said, was that people spent far too long producing elaborate and effective visual aids, and didn't think enough about the information. Have the answers to obvious questions been planned in advance? This shows an ability to think through a topic and predict areas of interest, both very useful attributes to any company.

The question of visual aids is a serious one. You want to show your knowledge of how they can be used effectively, but you are unsure about the equipment. This is where foresight is impressive: you ring and ask what will be available in the room on the day. The chances are that the answer will be the overhead projector, and you now know what type of visual material to prepare. Unless you are specifically asked to use a data projector, don't risk it. Too much can go wrong (see pages 128–30), and you have enough to worry about during your interview without extra problems of compatibility, using a strange laptop or taking too long to boot the whole system up. Prepare good quality overhead acetates, using colour if it's appropriate, and then you don't need to worry any further.

Nevertheless, the importance of preparing and rehearsing the presentation thoroughly, with your visual aids, can't be emphasized enough, if you are to show the appropriate management skills. For this reason, presentations have become increasingly important at all levels of the selection process – an applicant for a chief executive's post was told as soon as she appeared at the formal interview that she had been the only one of half a dozen experienced interviewees to keep to time in her presentation. She got the job.

> *Key point: if you have to give a presentation, prepare it carefully; think about likely questions.*

So you have a great deal of work to do in preparation for your second interview, which may start not with questions but with a dinner the night before. You may, of course, be told that this is not a part of the interview process, but you would do well to ignore such a comment; of course you will be assessed in an informal way during the evening. Nevertheless, try to behave as naturally as you can; be very polite and friendly to the other candidates; don't try to show off; don't drink too much; and don't relax so much that you aren't thinking about what you're saying. You need to show how well you can relate to strangers: ask about their interests or the place they come from, rather than just talking about yourself.

Such 'social' occasions can be a great strain, as can 'free' time during the next day, but it's useful to remember that everyone will feel the same way. The programme is likely to include a range of activities such as psychometric tests, group work, case studies and timed exercises, which are outside the scope of this book but not your careers advisors. Working in a group presents some difficulty, in that you want to make a mark, but not to be seen to dominate; being aware of this problem is at least halfway to solving it. If you feel that some stage of the programme has gone badly, don't allow yourself to lose confidence. It's unlikely that anyone has sailed through the whole day without some difficulty or self-doubt, and your worry may have been much less obvious to others than it was to you. Above all, don't give up. Even if you don't get this job, look on it as good experience for next time.

So at last you get to the interview itself, probably with a panel of three people. The advice about non-verbal behaviour which we gave earlier (see pages 142–5) still applies; believe that you've done well so far, and feel and look as confident as you can. This interview may well be very demanding, with some difficult questions and frequent 'what would you do if' scenarios. As before, if you don't know the answer, say so, but as far as you can, give thoughtful, reasoned responses. If you need time to think, ask for it. Don't show anxiety if you realize that you've given a poor answer. If you can think of a way to improve it, say 'I think I could express that better as ... ' or 'May I add to that answer ... ', but if you can't, let it go and continue to look and sound professional. Make eye contact as you answer: you may feel a bit as if you're under attack on all fronts, but the other candidates will have to face the same problems.

You won't be expected to know everything, and maintaining a professional relationship with the panel is of critical importance: don't let your answers ramble on, never become aggressive, even if you feel that a question is unfair (it might have been asked purely to see how you reacted), listen carefully to the questions and answer the one you are asked rather than the one you wish you had been asked. Remember that we suggested breathing exercises while you waited for your interview to start (see page 197). If there is a pause during the interview when the attention is off you (this often happens as one interviewer hands over to another for the next question), take as good a breath as you can without it being obvious, relax your shoulders, and let the breath out slowly. Nobody is likely to notice, but you will feel more in control as a result.

> *Key point: during your interview, give thoughtful, reasoned responses, don't rush your answers, and say if you don't know.*

As before, keep up the professionalism until the day is completely over, and don't allow yourself to be too discouraged, even if you feel that it didn't go well. You might have been much more impressive than you thought you were, and in any case, it was very good experience. If you don't get the job, you have nothing to lose by ringing the human resources person you met earlier and asking where the weaknesses were. You might get some good advice and a pointer for the future, and the person you speak to will be impressed by your thoroughness. You may also find that your call has another, totally unexpected, result: it sometimes happens that the chosen candidate turns the job down, and the company is still looking for a suitable employee, and who better than you, who took the trouble to ring?

> *Key point: don't relax until you are out of the room.*

This book has looked at communication in the wide variety of situations you may meet during your career as a student. This is perhaps the most important aspect of your course. If you lack specialist knowledge or expertise, that can be put right when it becomes necessary – in any case you are likely to have further training when you are at work. If you communicate well, during your course and at work, you have an invaluable tool in sharing your knowledge and commitment with friends, colleagues and, eventually, customers and clients; this may indeed be the basis of your success. Good luck!

Further Reading

Becker, Lucinda: *How to Manage your Arts, Humanities and Social Science Degree*, Palgrave Macmillan, 2002

Cottrell, Stella: *The Study Skills Handbook*, 2nd edn, Palgrave Macmillan, 2003

Cottrell, Stella: *Skills for Success*, Palgrave Macmillan, 2003

Greetham, Bryan: *How to Write Better Essays*, Palgrave – now Palgrave Macmillan, 2001

Peck, John and Coyle, Martin: *The Student's Guide to Writing*, Macmillan – now Palgrave Macmillan, 1999

Rose, Jean: *The Mature Student's Guide to Writing*, Palgrave – now Palgrave Macmillan, 2001

Index

A

abstracts, dissertation,
  see dissertations, abstracts
abbreviations 71–3, 75, 86
acknowledgements, dissertation,
  see dissertations,
  acknowledgements
active voice, passive voice 92–3
addresses in applications 170
American usage 67, 78
answering the question 37–9
apostrophes 65–6
appendices in reports 61
application forms
  checking 175
  honesty, need for 171–3
  personal choices 174–5
  personal information 170–4
  photocopies 168–9
  referees 169–70
  see also covering letters
applications online 182–3
assignment (first) 7–8
  see also essays
assessment
  continuous 155–6
  coursework 153–6
  examinations 155–6, 158–62
  see also revision, vivas

B

body language
  audience response 145–6
  cultural influence 142
  eye contact 112, 144–5
  facial expression 142
  feet 143–4
  first impressions 132–4, 142,
    144
  hands 142–3
  posture 143
  in telephoning 141
books, assessment of 21–3
  see also reading
brackets 86
breath control 137–8

C

CV
  checking 176, 179
  example 183–6
  format 176
  length 176
  referees 178
  see also covering letters
cards, *see* notes for
    presentations
Careers Advisory Service 167–8,
    190, 195, 203
careers fairs 191
checking
  dissertations 66–8
  visual aids 127
colons and semi-colons 81–2
commas 83–5
concluding a presentation,
    see presentations,
    conclusion
conclusions
  dissertations 61
  reports 53
confidence in speaking 107,
    136
  see also overconfidence
continuous assessment,
    see assessment
covering letters 171, 179–82
covering letter example 186–7
copyright, *see* references
curriculum vitae, *see* CV

D
dashes in punctuation 87
data projectors, *see* visual aids,
    specific
delivery in presentations,
    see voice
dissertations
    abstracts 64–5
    acknowledgements 60
    choice of subject 56–7
    objectives 57–9
    organization of material 57–8,
        60–1
    revision and checking
        66–8
    style 63–4
    timetable 59–60
    word allocation 61–2
distractions to
    listening 13–14

E
equipment for presentations,
    see visual aids, specific
essays
    essay planning 39–46
    long essays 49
examination techniques
    158–62
example CV, *see* CV, example
eye contact, *see* body
    language

F
file cards, *see* notes for
    presentations
font, in visual aids 121–2,
    125, 127
format
    dissertations 60–1
    reports 50–1
full stops 80–1

G
groups
    allocation of
        responsibilities 148
    handovers 149
    organization 133–4
    rehearsals 149–50
    small-group presentations
        97–104

H
handouts
    lectures 27
    presentations 119–20
Harvard system (of
    references) 29
headings
    dissertations 60–1
    reports 51–4
humour in presentations 139,
    146–7
hyphens 86

I
inclusive language 93
infinitives, split 90–1
Internet
    notes from 32–4
    use in job applications
        168, 200
    see also applications online
interviews
    careers fairs 191
    dress 197
    first and second 195–204
    preparation 190–3, 195–7
    presentations 201–3
    questions 195, 198–200
    telephone 194–5
    see also application forms,
        applications online, CV
introductions
    presentations 109
    reports 50–1

J
jargon 75

L
LCD projectors, *see* data
    projectors
lectures, note-taking,
    see note-taking
    from lectures
libraries, use of 5–6
listening
    barriers to 13–14
    positive 14–17
    preparation for 14–15
lists
    punctuation 81–2
    use 92

M
main body of reports 50
mature students 3–4, 154, 176, 177, 178, 196, 199
'milk round', see careers fairs

N
nerves
   control of 135–6, 138
   value 135
   see also confidence in speaking
non-verbal communication, see body language
notes for presentations
   content 117
   note cards 116–17
   visual aids 115–16
note-taking
   from CD-ROMs 34
   from the Internet 32–4
note-taking from lectures
   computer, use of 27–8
   preparation 25
   purpose 25–6
   recorded 27
note-taking from printed material
   formats 31–2
   plagiarism 28–30
   public domain material 30
   quotations 28–9
   references 29–30
   see also spider diagrams
numbering systems in reports 53–4

O
objectives
   dissertations 58–9
   note-taking 25–6
   readers 7, 18–19, 69
online applications, see applications online
organization of material, see spider diagrams
overconfidence 135
overhead projectors, see visual aids, specific

P
pace of speech in presentations 138–40

paragraphs 46–7, 92
part-time students 3
passive voice, see active voice, passive voice
plagiarisim 28, 30, 65–6
plural/singular agreement 91
PowerPoint presentations, see visual aids, spccific
prejudice in writing 93
presentation of assignments 48
presentations
   choice of topic 107
   conclusion 110
   delivery 137–41
   dress 132–3
   handovers 149
   humour 139, 146–7
   introduction 109
   language 112–15
   limitation of material 109–10
   middle section 109–10
   professionalism 107
   questions 110–11, 147–8
   rapport with audience 109, 135
   rehearsals 116, 118, 119, 136
   silence 138–40
   structure 108–10
   timing 118–19
   see also confidence, body language, groups, visual aids, voice, notes, handouts
punctuation 80–7
   see also commas, hyphens, etc

Q
questions, see presentations, questions

R
reading
   critical 19–20
   dangers of (in presentations) 112–15
   lists 17
   practice 24–5
   preparation 18–19
   purpose 18–19
   realistic 21
   skills 17–18
   speed 18
   writer's prejudice 20
   see also books, assessment of

recommendations in reports
  50–3
references 28–30
rehearsing presentations,
  see presentations, rehearsals
reports
  format 50–3
  presentation 53–4
  style 55
  summaries 54–5
research proposals 187–9
revision for examinations 156–8
  see also checking

S
semi-colons, *see* colons and
  semi-colons
seminars
  eye contact 145
  general 98–9
  guest speakers 103–4
  papers and presentations
    97–8
  student-led 99–103
sentences
  beginnings 89–91
  length 88–9
  structure 89–90
singular/plural agreement 91
spider diagrams (examples) 33,
  42, 43, 52
structure
  dissertations 57–8, 60–1
  presentations 108–10
  reports 50–3
studying effectively 5–7
style of writing
  abbreviations 71–3, 75
  active voice 92–3
  clichés 75
  context 70
  formal 71
  informal 72
  instructional 71
  jargon 75
  listening to style 94
  passive voice 92–3
  spoken 72

summaries in reports 54
supervisions, *see* tutorials

T
timing, *see* presentations, timing
tutorials 104–5

V
venue for presentations 133–4, 136
visual aids
  accuracy 127
  appropriate use 121
  as notes 115–16
  clarity 121–7
  colour 122, 127
  content 123–7
  examples 124 (poor), 126
    (improved)
  purpose 120–2
  quality 120
  rehearsal 127, 131
visual aids, specific
  data projectors 115, 122–3, 128–31
  handouts 119–20
  overhead projectors 125–8
vivas
  preparation and conduct 162–3
  purpose 163
voice
  emphasis 141
  exercises 137–8
  pace 138–40
  pauses 139–40
  variety 141
  volume 137–8

W
words
  accuracy 76–8
  American usage 78
  formality 74
  jargon 75
  new developments 79
  singulars and plurals 79
  see also style of writing
writing, *see* style of writing, words
writing and speaking, differences
    between 9–10